Great Colorado
BEAR
Stories

Laura Pritchett

RIVERBEND
PUBLISHING

*Dedicated to
James and Jake and Eliana
and to
wild bears and wild country and those
who embrace and protect both*

Editorial Note
In 2012 the Colorado Division of Wildlife, abbreviated as DOW, merged with the Division of Parks and Outdoor Recreation to become Colorado Parks and Wildlife, abbreviated as CPW. The new name and abbreviation are used in this book.

Great Colorado Bear Stories
© 2012 Laura Pritchett

ISBN 13: 978-1-60639-051-1

Printed in the United States of America.

1 2 3 4 5 6 7 8 9 SB 18 17 16 15 14 13 12

All rights reserved. No part of this book may be reproduced, stored, or transmitted in any form or by any means without the prior permission of the publisher, except for brief excerpts for reviews.

Cover design by Sarah E. Grant
Text design by Barbara Fifer
Front cover photo: Wild black bear by Donald M. Jones, Great Gray Imagery,
    www.donaldmjones.com
Back cover photo: Wild black bear in a tree in West Glenwood, Colorado,
    by Kevin Wright

Riverbend Publishing
P.O. Box 5833
Helena, MT 59604
1-866-787-2363
www.riverbendpublishing.com

Contents

Preface 5
The Ghost of Hope 11
The Wiseman Bear 23
Falling for Grizzlies 33
Being Good to Bears 41
Fast Grizzly Facts 51
Fast Black Bear Facts 55
Crawling into the Den 57
Firm in the Faith of the Wilderness 63
The Thin Line 69
Reported Colorado Bear Attacks on Humans 77
Sanctuary 103
Kwiyaga 109
Zebulon Pike's Arrest 115
The First Death 121
Old Mose 123
The President's Hunt 133
A Colorado Bear Hunt 143
The Best Historical Newspaper Stories 161
The Journal of a Trapper 181
Contemporary Stories from Around the State 185
Bear vs. Germ 203
Winner, Hands Down 209
The Beck Factor 222
Beyond Bear Aware 229
Basic Bear Smarts 238

Acknowledgments

Many people took time from busy lives to share stories and information, and to welcome me into their bear-savvy lives. Indeed, writing this book has been an exercise in getting to know some of the finest, wisest, toughest, and coolest people in this state, and I'm grateful our paths crossed.

Bryan Peterson, of Bear Smart Durango, not only listened to me think through the book, but also put me in touch with the right people, who then helped further. Special thanks go to Kevin Wright, Tom Beck, Jorge Andromidas, David Lewis, Eryn Mills, Peter Anderson, Dave Petersen, Patrick Finan, Sharon Baruch-Mordo, Dennis Schutz, Jeff Stephenson, Tim Schuett, Lisa Wolfe, John Broderick, Stewart Breck, Nanci Limbach, Al King, Matthew Box, Aaron Abeyta, Andy Sovick, Terry Campbell, Eric Hermann, Mark Schoenecker, Rose Bayless, Gail Marshall, and especially Al McClelland.

Thanks also to those who helped me with the writing: Rose Brinks, Laura Resau, Carrie Visintainer, Sarah Ryan, Dana Masden, Debbie Hayhow, and Molly Reid. May bears bless all librarians everywhere.

Finally, a big thanks to Chris Cauble for sending me on this adventure in the first place.

Preface

A bear kept me up last night. As I drifted off, I heard one banging up my neighbor's trash can, heard my chickens cackle in response, heard my dog get up from her bed to stand at the window and growl. This morning, when I walked outside, I saw that my yard swing had been clawed up—the green fabric remnants floated up in a small breeze. I glanced at my neighbor's trash can, now with a huge dent in the top, but otherwise still intact. Then I looked up, into the cottonwoods, scanning the crooks and big branches, just checking. Hoping, really.

I went for my usual walk, down the dirt county road in northern Colorado, along the first hogbacks of the Colorado Rockies. My breath misted out, the world was softly crystallized in white, the yellow dots of leaves circled through the air. The dog ran on ahead, sniffing; a fawn and doe stepped quietly out of sight. Mainly, though, I was looking down, scanning for scat—this time of year, there's bound to be a pile or two of apple-seed–laden stuff, crumbly and pleasant. Sure enough, I found several, and I paused in the quiet morning to gaze up at the foothills. Somewhere in the mountain mahogany, willows, wild plums, and rock outcroppings, a bear was hanging out.

This afternoon, at the bus stop, I will walk out and wait for my children—the mountain lions and bears are a little too prevalent right now, even for me. And tonight, probably, the phone will ring. This is the time of year my neighbors call each other: bring in your birdfeeders, watch your trash, did you see the cubs in the tree by the river? When we meet at the Grange, I will overhear someone complaining that she's got bear snot on her windowpanes.

Bears are a part of life here, but all I usually see is the evidence left behind. At my parents' ranch nearby, I recently walked out back to the far edge of the property—past the hay meadows and into wilder territory—and stopped under the hidden ancient apple trees surrounded in undergrowth. I marveled at the huge and plentiful piles of scat full of apple seeds, the clawed-off bark. When I moseyed back to the cluster of outbuildings, I found my parents gathered round the chicken house. They looked mildly grumpy: a bear and cubs had somehow twisted the window pane, and, without breaking the window, had broken into the supposedly-bear-proof chicken-house and slaughtered all the chickens. I stood there, surveying the damage, noticing the small paw prints—a mix of mud and chicken blood—that scaled a vertical cinderblock wall. Spider-man bears, I thought. I can't say that I was that sorry to have the rooster gone, because he'd harassed me for years, but the hens and chicks—well, that was a bummer. I mourned their loss and examined their entrails and feet scattered all around me. The big bear had also left us a scat pile as big as a full backpack that looked rather human (since the bear has been eating more like a human lately; chicken protein, for example), and we were fascinated by that, too. We wished the bears back into the wilderness, vowed to do better, and agreed that the bears should be full and content before heading into hibernation.

Such is our life with bears. We all do what we can to minimize bear-human conflict, we must try to do more, but sometimes events like this happen anyway, accepted by us all as part of the deal. And as I fall asleep tonight, I'll listen for evidence again, and be grateful, as always, that I live in the company of bears.

When I was asked to write this book, I hesitated. For one thing, I didn't know that much about bears—either the black bears that now occupy our state, or the grizzlies that once did (and perhaps still do). I'm an outdoorsperson, and I'd classify myself as a student of Colorado's backcountry and wildlife, but that made me no expert. But while it's true that writers often write what they know, it's equally true that writers write what they *want* to know—what they're curious about. And it's true I was curious about bears.

My other worries about writing a bear book were broader: I didn't want to write a romantic-sweet bear book. The bears of our cultural zeitgeist make me queasy—gift shops make me cringe, with bear-paw coffee mugs and stylized bears with Indian maidens scantily clad. The nearest restaurant/shop to me, in fact, has all this stuff, along with a stuffed bear cub standing with a sign in his paws: Please Seat Yourself, which you can do, and then stare at the jackalope on the wall.

Nor did I want to write a horror-thriller book about bears and their menacing ways. The other end of the cultural mythology is just as erroneous. Movies about human-eating-grizzlies and orphan-producing bears make me wonder why humans often wish to make wild animals into something far more dangerous than they actually are. Our grossly distorted perception of them seems very stubborn—perhaps an innate fear of predators contributes to this, even when there's ample evidence to suggest that only very rarely are we anything except the top of the food chain. In any case, it seems we've often been too busy killing these animals rather than observing them for the creatures that they are, and I certainly didn't want to contribute to that cultural mythology.

So why write a book about the best bear stories of Colorado? In the end, because of one reason: curiosity is one definition of love. The more I learned about real bears, the more I loved bears. Not in the hug 'em goofy sense, but in the deep respect and care that goes along with real emotion.

My hope, then, has been to paint the real portrait of bears. I am not here to reveal bears as dangerous creatures, although, yes, both black bears and grizzlies can be dangerous, and in this book there are some stories of tragedy and violence. Nor am I presenting them as cute cuddly things, although that famous photograph of Theodore Roosevelt bottle-feeding a bear is awfully endearing, and the cubs I've seen surely make one want to cuddle. But in the end, bears are what they are—wild animals, full of curiosity, strength, playfulness, boredom, activity. I wanted to get to know them and the people who have—by choice or not—found their lives intersecting with the bruins of Colorado.

One epiphany that came with writing this book was the full realization of how many grizzlies once roamed the space where I live—and for the first time, I felt the sorrow and silence of their absence (and the safety I take for granted, perhaps—although I also came to fear grizzlies far less after learning more). Some of the chapters explore the first encounters with these grizzlies, from the most famous Colorado grizzly, Old Mose, to the quiet playful ones in the land of Enos Mills, who was perhaps their best advocate. "It would be a glorious thing," he wrote in 1919, "if every one appreciated the real character of the grizzly bear."

This book also explores the possibility of a remnant population of grizzlies in Colorado, and the more I talked to people in the know, the more I became open to the idea that there might, in fact, still be a chance that some exist, though not in any numbers to remain a viable population. I also interviewed others who would like grizzlies to be a part of Colorado's future—a concept that I find fascinating for the deep wildness and hope that such a goal represents. Historical documents proved to be equally interesting, as when I discovered a nutty story about Zebulon Pike and the first grizzlies on public exhibition in the world, or when I discovered early newspaper accounts of grizzlies that were charming, horrific, or downright funny.

I also learned a lot about Colorado's black bears, *Ursus*

americanus. If the grizzly is indeed extinct, black bears (which can vary in color and are often not black) are the largest carnivores in the state. There are an estimated 10,000 to 12,000 of them here, and thus bear stories are pretty common around the campfire and water cooler. Although black bears still occupy vast areas of North America, bears have lost 90 percent of their original range, and humans continue to encroach on what remains of bear habitat (consider, for example, that condos are often placed at the same altitude as bear habitat). It's not surprising, then, that conflicts between bears and humans have increased dramatically in the last few decades. In fact, these conflicts are related to a third of all bear mortalities in Colorado—and a few tragic encounters for people, too.

In researching this book, I have crawled into a black bear's den and put my face up to a hibernating (and tranquilized) black bear, watched baby black bear cubs play, gone exploring in the far reaches of Colorado for stories. I have talked to a father who lost a son; two men who nearly lost their lives; and scientists who have spent hundreds of hours with hundreds of black bears. I have talked to historians, artists, good hunters and moronic hunters. Across the state (there are even black bears on the plains of Colorado), I've listened to stories. Thus, this book is about bears, but it is also a story of people; there cannot be one without the other. It is also very much a story about place—some of the very far corners and highest reaches of my home state of Colorado.

Bears seize our imagination, perhaps because they are so human. We seek them out and integrate them into our lives in all sorts of ways. Tourists want a glimpse; schools use bears as symbols of identity; scientists study; conservationists worry; wildlife officials deal with the human-bear interface; hunters want to harvest the animals for sport, trophy, meat, or pelt; photographers hope for the right light, the right bear, the right moment; Native Americans associate the animals with spiritual beings, death, and rebirth; many others feel a spiritual or soulful pull. And all of us, I think, would pause and marvel if, by chance, a bear sauntered into sight.

Despite the fascination, though, few of us have had the opportunity to really get to know bears—they are by nature reclusive and quiet creatures. It's fair to say that I spend a lot of time outside in the mountains—hiking or cross-country skiing or snowshoeing or camping—and I have to admit that I haven't seen that many bears. When I have, it's usually been a quick glimpse, save for the times when a bear is up in a tree and stuck there. For that reason, perhaps, I didn't know that much about their habitat and habits, their role in ecosystems, and about the people who know them best. The greatest gift in writing this book was that I've come to know the bear as more than a creature that rips up my lawn furniture or beats up neighbor's trash cans. Their habits, their preoccupations, their physiology, their personalities have—at least a little—been opened to me.

It is perhaps the case that once you start to know a creature, you can fall in love, and if you fall in love, you want to protect. Thus, the final lesson for me in writing this book is the renewed conviction and belief that this great state has the great gift of bears—and therefore the deep responsibility of keeping them safe and their habitat wild. Our record thus far hasn't been stellar—from the extermination of grizzlies to the current bear-human interface problems—but the fact that Colorado has bear stories to tell offers hope. There are real and tangible things we can do to protect them and their wilderness. And the best way to do that, perhaps, is to know their stories. This book contains, then, the best stories I could find. Enjoy!

THE GHOST OF HOPE

GRIZZLIES IN COLORADO

PERHAPS THEY'RE HERE, deep in the mountains of southwest Colorado. Perhaps they're all gone, shot and trapped and poisoned to extinction. Perhaps they should be reintroduced. Or perhaps there is not enough wildness in the lands of Colorado to protect them.

Grizzlies in Colorado. They used to be here, in the hundreds, and their current existence remains just at the cusp of possibility. Rumors abound, sightings are reported, searches are conducted. The subject spawns all sorts of emotions, depending on who you talk to: hope or sorrow, relief or disdain, believers and doubters. Many will argue that grizzlies have been extinct in Colorado for decades; that for better or worse, they're gone. And yet, deep in the southern Colorado mountains, in the San Juan Mountains, there's just enough wildness left for the possibility, enough evidence to fuel the fires of hope.

WHEN I TRAVEL through the southwest part of the state, into folds of mountains that repeat to the horizon, it's no surprise that the existence of grizzlies in Colorado is not a cut-and-dried situation. The scope of the landscape is enormous and, no matter which side of the debate you fall on, it's true that there's room—as evidenced in these mountains themselves—for a little uncertainty.

While grizzlies were all gone from northern Colorado by the 1920s, viable populations were still present in the southern part of the state until much later. In 1952, a government trapper named Lloyd Anderson—who had already legally killed at least seven grizzlies and an estimated five hundred black bears—killed a sow in this area. This sow was later deemed the last grizzly in Colorado, and wildlife officials declared the grizzly extinct statewide. Around the same time, the state of Colorado formed the "Rio Grande–San Juan Grizzly Bear Management Area" to protect grizzlies—meaning that, ironically enough, by the time that the Colorado Wildlife Commission declared the grizzly bear endangered, it was too late.

Most people believed that the law was moot anyway—there weren't any grizzlies left to protect. But then, in 1979, something incredible happened: a hunting outfitter named Ed Wiseman, who was bow hunting for elk, killed an old female grizzly in the south San Juans. This was *twenty-seven years* after they'd been declared extinct.

The "Wiseman Bear," as she was commonly called, stirred up the debate. For years, reports and rumors about grizzly bears had been surfacing—but this was proof. In response to the Wiseman bear, Colorado Parks and Wildlife (CPW) took another look, and a study was headed by its well-known and respected black bear biologist, Tom Beck. Beck spent two summers directing a search for grizzlies in the San Juans, and while the so-called "Beck Study," turned up "lots of black bears but no grizzlies," Beck also noted in his final report that "failure to catch a grizzly does not mean a definite absence of bears."

In fact, Beck, now retired, knows that there were grizzlies in the state in between the 1950s and 1970s. "What it's hard to convince people of is that while grizzly bears weren't being killed, it doesn't mean they weren't there," he told me. "The state had said that was illegal to kill a grizzly, but if you were setting traps, how were you going to release one? People didn't have the drugs or the know-how to immobilize bears yet. So what was a guy to do if he caught one? Shoot it and not report it. I asked a number of sheep men, none of whom I will identify, and trappers, none of whom I will identify, if this indeed happened. All of them confirmed [it]. So, there were bears here during that interim time. Not a lot. But they were here."

Which just makes the question more interesting: Was the Wiseman bear the last one, or not? Besides having unreported deaths, many people believe that just because grizzlies are smart enough to avoid notice, doesn't mean they aren't there. In fact, that particular attribute might be the very thing that keeps them alive.

Just ask rancher and guide Dennis Schutz. He told me that he watched a large grizzly sow and three cubs for about half an hour in 1990. "I'm positive they were grizzlies," he said. "I was up on the mountain, in an area I'd never been before, and I was looking for a way out before it got dark. I found a big elk trail that I knew would take me out, so I stopped to relax, and was sitting still when the bears came out." As it turns out, this area was about only about a mile away from where the Wiseman bear was killed—and she was, according to some, a lactating sow.

Schutz recounted how he watched three bears came out into a meadow while he was resting, and he thought, "Man, those are big black bears." But then they did something odd—they started playing. "It was like a slug fest going on," he said. "They were romping and rolling, having a big time in the middle of a grassy meadow. Three adult black bears, acting like cubs—that was odd. Then all the sudden, in a creek bed filled with alders, a bear comes out of the creek bottom. And she was a lot bigger than the cubs. She must have known I was there—I don't know if she scented me or sensed me or what. But she got them out of there. She smacked a couple of them and took off leading them up the hill. When one stopped to play, she made a little circle around him and barked him into shape. As they left, she would stop and sit on her haunches and lean back to her left and look me in the eye."

Schutz contacted Colorado Parks and Wildlife (CPW) right away. "It was elk season, and the local officers were busy, and it was several days before they were able to go up there. There was some snow on the ground on the north-facing steep canyon. There were obvious bear tracks, and there had been some elk in there, and the tracks were sort of melted out. The CPW said it was interesting but inconclusive."

Whether or not people believe him is not one of Schutz's main concerns. "I don't care if people believe me or not. Some do, some don't. Those were grizzlies. We're talking about 68,000 acres of private and undisturbed land. There are places here that I bet have never been touched by a human foot. There's just no reason that they can't be up there. And I have a good feeling that I'm telling truth. It makes me happy inside knowing that they're up there."

A HANDFUL OF PEOPLE, guided by hope and instinct, perhaps, have gone looking for exactly that—evidence that Colorado is still wild enough to have some of her original grizzlies. Everyone who keeps up with such things knows who they are—they are Colorado legends. Perhaps the most colorful is Doug "Hayduke" Peacock, a filmmaker, author, outdoorsman, and grizzly expert. He's been looking for evidence of bears for years, and has written extensively about his inquiries and searches for grizzly, including the popular book *In the Presence of Grizzlies,* in which he and his wife Andrea delve into the life of grizzlies and grizzly-human relationship via interviews with biologists, mauling victims, hunters, and photographers. Peacock believes that the existence of a small population of grizzlies in Colorado has been clearly demonstrated, citing hair samples collected by searchers and identified by an independent forensics laboratory as grizzly; several finds of huge, grizzly-like tracks; and two highly-credible sightings. What he wants is to prove the existence of a remnant population of native Colorado grizzlies and assure their preservation.

Several expeditions to look for evidence have been mounted. In September 1990, Doug Peacock, writer Rick Bass, and biologist Dennis Sizemore went on a trip in search of evidence. Bass's book *The Lost Grizzlies* is a detailed account of that trip and the possibility of grizzlies in general, or perhaps the possibility that there is simply enough wildness to contain them. "I am not arguing for bears, because that cannot really be done," Bass wrote. "They seem beyond argument, like whales or clouds. What I am arguing for is a little space for the bears." Recently, I asked Bass about the possibility of bears since the publication of his book. "The world has gotten smaller since Doug and I were in the San Juans," he said. "My own feelings are that they are gone for now—but that one way or the other, they will be back. I look forward to that day."

David Petersen, a well known outdoorsman and writer from the area, has also been on the lookout—and echoes Bass's sentiments. He believes that the last credible report occurred well into the 90s. "The last report of a live grizzly in Colorado that I find credible was the DeSwarte encounter in the summer of 1995," he told me. As he notes in his book *Ghost Grizzlies: Does the Great Bear Still Haunt Colorado?,* this bear sighting was later judged a "Class 3" by Tom Beck, who investigated the report, meaning that one physical characteristic of a grizzly bear was reported by a credible witness, but that no other evidence was discovered.

Petersen has conducted his own extensive searches, and his wonderful book recounts four years of trips into the backcountry, interviewing wildlife officials, hikers, hunters, taxidermists, and anyone else with a connection to the great bear—hoping to find evidence that a few still range Colorado's rugged backcountry. His book is a thorough and lively account of evidence and the country itself.

"If any native grizzlies remain in Colorado," he told me, "I have come to hope they are never discovered. I am a passionate traditional bowhunter. Yet I do not hunt bears. While I have no objection to fair-chase hunting of bears (that is, no bait and no hounds involved) as a necessary element of scientific wildlife management, and while I've eaten bear meat and find it delicious, I simply have no desire to hunt bears myself. If you explore the worldwide history of man's relationship to bears, you'll find a remarkable consistency in the shared feeling that bears are 'almost us.' Indeed, it's a universal human 'spiritual thing.' Basically, I quit arguing for reintroduction, called off my own search, and suggest we should just let any remaining bears die in dignified peace, since the political situation in this state will never accommodate wild grizzlies." He notes that CPW (and others, including himself) continue to get grizzly sighting reports every tourist season, some with photos. "None so far, zero, has been in the least credible," he said. "In short, while I cannot say 'no more grizzlies in Colorado,' I am frankly doubtful."

And yet the debate rages on. Some people liken the possibility of grizzlies in Colorado as being along the lines of "Yup, I fished for the Loch Ness Monster and I saw a grizzly being chased by a Yeti," as one CPW employee humorously put it. But reports continue to trickle in. One credible sighting came when a plane crashed at Banded Peaks, where searchers believe they found grizzly tracks in snow near the wreckage. From the air, they appeared to be snowshoe tracks. Another report came in 2006, when two hunters say they spotted a female grizzly bear and two cubs near Independence Pass. They were experienced hunters, and there was enough evidence to take the report seriously—the Parks and Wildlife officials used a helicopter with videographers and photographers on board. They searched the area but found no evidence to substantiate the report.

The mystery remains—which is, perhaps, the best way to leave something as grand as the grizzly.

WHETHER OR NOT they're here, some wonder if they should be back. One such person is Jorge Andromidas, who founded the Colorado Grizzly Project in 1995. This group advocates reintroduction either to augment a small population which may still exist in the San Juan ecosystem—or to re-establish one using bears from a similar habitat in the interior West. In addition, Andromidas also argues that the time has come for responsible management agencies to act as if grizzlies were still present, and to take immediate action to protect Colorado's last few grizzlies and their habitat. After all, should the existence of a distinct southern Rockies grizzly subspecies be proven, it would be the most critically endangered mammal in North America. His group would also like to see sheep allotments purchased and retired by groups like the Nature Conservancy; or, to have the Forest Service retire them when the current permit holders no longer want them. They'd also like to carefully regulate black bear hunting in the area where grizzlies would be introduced, since it's very hard to tell a black bear from a grizzly.

The Colorado Grizzly Project, he noted, "was intended

to build tolerance for grizzlies among that segment of the population that would otherwise be adamantly opposed to re-introduction." To that end, they want to instill a "recognition of the value of a whole, healthy, and intact ecosystem" and to "create or sustain an appreciation of the grizzly bear as a top-level predator." One of his main goals is simply to "build a constituency for the grizzly, and that comes with patience," he told me, noting that successful lynx and wolverine (and possibly wolf) reintroduction might pave the way, as people learn that these animals are not the dangerous killing creatures they were once made out to be. "I don't think it's in the best interest of anyone to haul bears to the San Juans without having done further habitat study and education of the local populace. But people might come to recognize that top-level predators like the grizzly bear still have not only relevance, but a distinct physical place in Colorado, particularly in the southwest."

He'd also like to convince people that the existence of grizzly bears would not harm the local economy, but would help it. "As the economic viability of ranch work declines, tours and outdoor activities offer an economic alternative. Whether it's Japanese tourists or people getting on a horse to ride up into the San Juans, people have an interest in the real world. They have an interest in non-consumptive use of resources—there's been a transition from a consumptive use of the wilderness to a more sustainable model. I want people to know that we have one foot in the real world, one foot in the ideal."

In fact, his role in moderating public opinion on grizzlies is in response to extreme positions on both sides—not only bear alarmists, but bear enthusiasts. Timothy Treadwell, the filmmaker who lived among the grizzlies in Alaska for thirteen years before getting killed by a grizzly, contacted Andromidas "wanting approval of his views and practices—

wanting an endorsement of his goals, more or less." Andromidas, however, refused: "I warned him and told him, 'You're not doing anything good for the bears, and you're endangering yourself.'" Andromidas made it clear that he doesn't want to anthropomorphize bears, or romanticize them—and he doesn't want others too, either.

But his work on and about bears has given him a sense of place, a sense of the ecological niche bears fill, and the integrity of whole ecosystems. He added that we don't exactly know what ecological values grizzlies bring to ecosystems (although he's also hesitant to use that term at all, because it tends to reduce wild creatures to the level of economic assets rather than creatures with intrinsic worth). He did note, however, that grizzlies are seed dispersers, they aerate soil as they vigorously dig for marmots and field mice and roots, and that their consumption of rodents may help regulate those populations.

It would be hard to be a grizzly advocate without getting curious about their possible existence, and Andromidas has gone looking himself. He was a field researcher on the Citizens Search for the Colorado Grizzly project, which was a concerted, diligent effort to find a sign of grizzlies. The Wiseman Bear, he noted, was a female, and appeared to have borne young. "I was invited to examine the pelt of the Wiseman grizzly at what is now the Denver Museum of Nature and Science, and the teats displayed signs of having been used by nursing cubs. Which means there was a male to impregnate her, and at least one or two cubs. With the sightings and such excellent habitat, there was a likelihood that grizzlies could have endured."

He added that the habitat of that region is excellent. "Some people say that the habitat is better than that in Yellowstone. I'm not a scientist, but I can see why. Consider the remoteness—less oil and gas drilling, fewer people, less hunting pressure. Also, good precipitation, good food sources." Such a population would be an "island population"—cut off from others—but Andromidas pointed out that "Yellowstone is too, and Glacier is on the threshold of becoming an island population, because of development in Alberta."

His search did turn up interesting clues—he noted that over 1,000 hair samples and bear scat were collected, but as far as he knows, the items were never tested—a bit of a mystery in itself, noting that "as far as I know, those samples just deteriorated." The search also revealed differing opinions about what should be done *should* a bear be discovered. Although there was agreement and camaraderie among the bear-seekers about finding a bear, there has been some conflict about what to do immediately after. "Even back at that time, there was a split—a schism between people who wanted to find incontrovertible evidence and who wanted that evidence reported to the officials," he told me. "And there were others who thought we should just protect that bear—not even report it—and let the bear live out its life, without all that radio collaring, extracting a molar, blood draws, and all the inevitable handling of that bear."

This brought up perhaps the most intriguing point of the case for grizzlies in Colorado. As Andromidas hinted, there are certainly people who might be seeing bears, but keeping mum. Indeed, while talking to various people in southern Colorado, I got the distinct impression that some people weren't telling me the whole story—and I got the impressions that sightings are more common than one would think. Schutz, the ranch manager and guide who spotted the three bears, confirmed my suspicion. He said, "If I had it to do over, I would just tell my friends. I'd keep quiet, more or less. I didn't know then that speaking up would cause a semi-stampede of people who wanted to see them. I'm a different person now." Then he paused and chuckled a little. "If

I saw them again—or if I've *seen* them again—well, now, I wouldn't say." And indeed, perhaps it's best to leave it that way, in the hopes that wildness can remain wild.

THE WISEMAN BEAR

AND THE NATURAL HISTORY
OF THE GRIZZLY

IN A QUIET back room at the Denver Museum of Nature and Science, Jeff Stephenson shepherded me through a maze of army-green lockers and shelves, and then handed me a surprisingly bright pair of purple latex gloves. Since he was the Collections Manager in charge of zoology, I assumed he wanted to protect his specimens, and that the oil on my hands wouldn't be doing them any favors. But as it turned out, he was protecting me, too: he explained that arsenic was once used for preserving animals, and although the practice stopped years ago, there was enough left to consider the whole collection mildly contaminated.

Convinced, I put the bright gloves on. I was glad to avoid that danger in order to touch another—or, at least, to touch remains of an animal that once was. I was eager to touch the famous "Wiseman bear," not because this last known grizzly of Colorado had such powerful and deadly potential (although she nearly did kill Ed Wiseman in her last minutes), but because of the secrets she might hold. Mysteries, perhaps, can also be rife with hidden danger.

I reached out to touch her. The Wiseman bear's pelt was folded on a table in front of me, her skull and bones resting next to her pelt, large and human-like. I ran my hand across her massive head, down her brown-with-black-stripe pelt, over her short rounded ears, and then across the broad grizzly shoulders. Her teeth were yellow and large, as were her claws. I unfolded her hide so that I could see her chest, and I fingered the two wounds, one of which killed her.

"I suppose that's what did it," Stephenson said, putting words to what I was thinking: *This is the wound that took the last known grizzly in Colorado—this small hole left a larger hole in our state. She lost this fight, and we lost too.*

It was deserted and quiet in this back room—we were away from the schoolchildren visiting that day, away from the fiberglass replica of the T. Rex at the entrance, away from the Pirate exhibit. As we quietly stared at the bear, Stephenson told me about the role of the museum, which, as he said, is "to record the natural and cultural artifacts and to be the warehouse of the vouchers of that story."

Thank heavens for museums, of course, for doing exactly that—but it also strikes me that some stories can't be known. This bear, for instance, has spurred a lively debate and even a federal investigation, and the true story can't be known for sure, except, perhaps, by one man—Ed Wiseman. What actually happened that day? How did the grizzly die? That particular story comes down to a he-said, she-said type of story, but behind that story is another, larger story. The story of human nature, our defense mechanisms, our desire and ability to kill, and our decisions whether or not to. And that's the story that I really find intriguing.

THE GRIZZLY BEAR has been on the North American continent for 200,000 years, and is thought to descend from the brown bear, *Ursus arctos*, which crossed to Alaska from eastern Russia across the Bering Land Bridge. Over time, America's brown bear developed distinctive characteristics and became what we know today as the grizzly bear, or *Ursus arctos horribilis*. Tens of thousands of years later, grizzlies were joined in North America by the earliest human migrants to the Pacific Northwest. The link between Native American cultures and the great bears has been well established—to my knowledge, all American Indian tribes in bear territory placed great importance on the bear, who was viewed as both capable of great danger and as having great spiritual and regenerative powers.

It's thought that the first European to specifically mention bears was Francesco Vasquez de Coronado, whose journal of 1540 makes a comment, although he doesn't go into detail (his travels, by the way, took him as far north as present-day Colorado). Probably the first serious mention of the grizzly by a European was that of Father Antonio de la Ascensión, official scribe on the voyage of Sebastian Vizcaino. In 1602, the padre saw the bears feeding on a beached whale and, later inspecting their tracks in the sand, noted that they measured "a good third of a yard long and a hand wide."

In 1666, Claude Jean Allouez, a French missionary, described a nation of Native Americans who are "eaten by bears of frightful size, all red, and with prodigiously long claws." Grizzlies were next mentioned by English explorer Henry Kelsey, who, in 1691, wrote of "a great sort of Bear wch is Bigger than any white Bear & is Neither White nor Black But silver hair'd like our English Rabbit."

At the time of the Lewis and Clark expedition in the early 1800s, grizzly numbers in the future Lower 48 were estimated at 50,000 to 100,000. Lewis and Clark may not have been the first white men to encounter grizzly bears, but their 1803-1806 trip across the West had the unique and unprecedented mission, which was to scientifically describe the flora and fauna of country. Thus, they became the first to use direct field observations to describe the grizzly bear, as well as the first to acquire a full specimen for study. In 1805, Lewis and Clark were heading west along the Missouri River when they encountered two grizzly bears, which they fired upon. In his journal entry for that day, Lewis compared the grizzly to the well-known black bear, noting that "it is a much more furious and formidable animal, and will frequently pursue the hunter when wounded." Indeed, Lewis was the first naturalist to encounter a grizzly, and his account became the new standard.

Other accounts quickly followed: In 1807, explorer Lieutenant Zebulon Pike sent two live grizzly bear cubs to President Thomas Jefferson, and these became the first grizzlies ever put on public display in the world. In 1814, DeWitt Clinton published a thesis on the grizzly bear based almost entirely on Lewis's field observations and the specimen he had brought back from his trip, which helped pave the way for the animal's official classification. The Hayden Geological Survey in the 1870s was the first federally-funded geological survey to explore and document features—and although the expedition focused on geology, Hayden also added to the knowledge of animals, including bears. In a 1930s scientific paper, for instance ("Grizzly Bears of Colorado," by Edward R. Warren), there is a notation that Hayden collected a grizzly in Colorado, catalogued in 1873.

What came next is well known: the grizzly bear population declined dramatically. Several factors contributed to their demise: increasing human population, the invention of the cartridge rifle, the cultural zeitgeist of grizzly-as-dangerous and the glorification of hunting, and above all else, the government's dictate that grizzlies be removed. Although a few radical voices, such as Enos Mills, argued for the preservation of bears and/or the re-consideration of bear behavior, these voices went largely unheard. Grizzly bears were vigorously sought out and killed by European settlers in the 1800s and early 1900s—in fact, all big game animals began a steep decline: elk nearly vanished, and antelope were reduced greatly in number. Bounties were paid for dead grizzles, and Colorado had a state policy to kill the bears.

The decline was fast: Between 1850 and 1920 grizzly bears were eliminated from 95 percent of their original range, first on the Great Plains and later in remote mountainous areas. Unregulated killing of bears continued in most places through the 1950s and resulted in a further 52 percent decline in their range between 1920 and 1970. By the mid-19th century, killing by ranchers and government trappers had reduced Colorado's grizzlies to a few shy survivors, and the grizzly was listed as a threatened species in the Lower 48 states in 1975 under the Endangered Species Act. Today, the U.S. Fish and Wildlife Service counts between 1,200 and 1,400 wild grizzly bears in the West. None, according to officials, reside in Colorado.

But the mountains of Colorado, particularly the San Juan Mountains of southwestern Colorado, hold some of the richest grizzly habitat in North America—and the bears were once ubiquitous in our state.

And that's precisely where this bear—and her story—come from.

WITH MY PURPLE-GLOVED HANDS, I dug my fingers into the presumed-last-grizzly-bear's hide. Her fur was thick and beautiful, even all these years after her death. I picked up her paws, looked at the broken claws. Stephenson pointed out an abscessed tooth and the wearing on her teeth. We looked at her nipples, which were distended and showed possible signs of nursing (important, because it means there was a male to impregnate her, and cubs that possibly outlived her). But more than anything, he pointed out the arthritis on her thoracic spine.

"This is arthritic lipping," he told me. "This bear was in a lot of pain. I don't guess that she was moving around much. Look, here," he said, pointing to a joint, "and here and here. Look at all that arthritis. This bear..." and with that, he trailed off.

We were both thinking of her demise—because what this bear did—or didn't do—has been the subject of much debate and local lore.

No one disputes the fact that she had two wounds—one in her lower throat, one in the chest area. The mystery comes down to one question: Who attacked whom? The brief version of the story is this: Ed Wiseman contended that while he was hunting elk in September of 1979, the bear charged him and, in self defense, he stabbed the bear with a hand-held arrow. There is no doubt that he was severely mauled by the bear, but others think that Wiseman or his hunting client illegally shot the bear first.

The most in-depth account of the event appears in the book *Ghost Grizzlies* by David Petersen, who went with Wiseman to the site and heard the story there. According to this account, Wiseman recalled first seeing the bear as it was charging him and hollering "No!" while he put up his bow as a shield. The bear, however, never broke its run. "In a flash it was on me," Wiseman told Petersen, "slapping the bow out of my hand." The bear bit into his leg and shook him, then turned and grabbed his right shoulder. Blood was everywhere. "Then I spotted one of the arrows that had been knocked out of my bow quiver...So I reached out and grabbed the arrow with my left hand, rolled over on my back and stabbed upward." He doesn't remember the rest of the fight, although he remembers knowing he was going to stab the bear a second time. He also remembers blood spurting all over him, watching the bear walk away, seeing her put her left paw on a log, and rest her chin on the paw—which was how she died.

The situation was nearly fatal. The man Wiseman was with built a fire, left for help, got lost (losing several critical hours), and returned later. A helicopter flew in, and the pilot feared it was too late—Wiseman was too torn up, had lost too much blood, and was hypothermic. Wiseman was flown to Alamosa Community Hospital, where a lengthy recovery started.

A federal investigation also began—mandated by the Endangered Species Act. The bear was necropsied at Colorado State University, but this was after ten days, and a lot of disintegration had occurred. The first wound, in the throat, was determined not to have been fatal; the second, to the chest, was fatal and appeared to be from a sharp flat instrument, like a knife blade—the official report ruled out its having been possible with a hand-held arrow, as Wiseman claimed. Petersen, however, noted that Wiseman's arrows were tipped with Bear Razorheads and can account for the wound pattern, and noted further that Wiseman's strength and fitness at that time allowed him to strike the bear that hard with a hand-held arrow. Many people testified as to Wiseman's good and credible character, and, perhaps most importantly to the case, Wiseman (and his client) both passed a polygraph test. Wiseman was cleared—but the debate has raged on.

On one hand, as I looked at the evidence of painful arthritis, it seemed unlikely that this bear would have charged *any*thing. On the other hand, as Petersen noted, perhaps it was the grizzly's advanced age and physical disabilities that weakened her attack, and allowed Wiseman's narrow victory. Who am I to know? The only thing I was certain of, as I fingered the holes in her hide, was that this old female grizzly went down fighting—and that, the larger scope of things—this bear had suffered what every other grizzly in Colorado had.

When I was done looking at the Wiseman bear, Stephenson showed me the other bear skulls in this back room (as with most museums, only about 0.2 percent of the Denver Museum of Nature and Science's holdings are on display at once—the rest of the cool stuff is stored in great rooms like this). There were shelves of skulls of all kinds of bears—polar, black, grizzly—all carefully labeled and lined up, each housing a story.

Stephenson then wandered off down an aisle and showed me species that have gone totally extinct. In several drawers were passenger pigeons, some with beautiful pink chests, and their eggs. Another drawer revealed ivory-billed woodpeckers. There were also Carolina parakeets, and I examined the tag on one of the legs, with old-fashioned careful cursive writing, which read: "July 1882 Cherokee Nation—Indian Territory." Then it was off to other things—he showed me part of the collection of dung beetles (Denver has the second largest collection in the country) and also Voda's skeleton (Voda was the Denver Zoo's polar bear that gave birth to the famous Klondike and Snow), and talked about their mammal and bird frozen-tissue repository.

"I have the best job in Colorado," Stephenson told me, as we left the back room. I could tell he wasn't kidding—he looked like a proud father in charge of these rare specimens. "My job's about documenting, preserving, and teaching about the story of life," he added. "Sometimes that means recording the last of a species; other times the first known occurrence."

He (reluctantly, it seemed) took me upstairs, into the public part of the museum. Schoolchildren ran around, a museum worker dressed as a pirate waved her sword at me. On the second floor, however, we came to relative quiet: here were the old familiar dioramas of bears, looking about the same as they did in my childhood.

In several cases were groups of grizzlies, which spawned a quick discussion of that term—grizzly—and how it came to be. The term "grizzly bear" supposedly refers to "grizzled" or gray hairs in its fur, but when naturalist George Ord formally named the bear in 1815, he misunderstood the word as "grisly," thus producing its Latin name *horribilis*." The first explorer to describe the bear as "grizzled," in fact, was Englishman Samuel Hearne, who journeyed across northwestern Canada to the Arctic Ocean from 1769 to 1772. In his journal, Hearne mentioned seeing the "skin of an enormous grizzled Bear" and camping at a spot "not far from Grizzled Bear Hill, which takes its name from the number of those animals that are frequently known to resort thither…"

At one point, Theodore Roosevelt tried to get the spelling of "grizzly" changed to "grisly," suggesting that "the name of this bear has reference to its character, and not its color." He conceded, however, that perhaps the spelling "grizzly" was "too well established to be now changed."

Indeed, as I looked at the display of grizzlies, I noted that these particular ones looked neither grizzled (they're quite brown) or nor grisly but, either way, the term "grizzly" was stuck in my mind.

"No matter what you call them, at least they're out there somewhere," I told Stephenson.

"I know it," Stephenson said, and then added, "They're not extinct yet. I would really like to have been able to watch a live dodo or learn the habits of a Tasmanian wolf. Grizzly bears may be gone from Colorado, but at least we still have them on the planet. Fortunately."

And with that, Stephenson and I parted ways—he back to his room of specimens, me to the mountains of Colorado. On the way out, underneath the T. Rex, I stopped to think about the Wiseman. Back in the 1980s, the Denver Museum of Nature and Science used to have a display of the Wiseman grizzly's hide and skull and fatal arrow on display. It's since been replaced by dioramas, but I'm glad that in the quiet corners of the museum, she's being kept for the citizens of Colorado and the nation. It's right to keep the evidence and story alive, to help us remember what we've lost.

Falling for Grizzlies

and Enos Mills

I'VE FALLEN IN LOVE with grizzlies. And as sometimes happens, I've fallen in love with my teacher, the one who sparked me alive, one Enos A. Mills. He died nearly a hundred years ago, but it doesn't matter: I'm smitten. He seems to be the human who knew Colorado grizzlies the best, and probably spent more quality time with them than any other. He's also the man who helped me really know them—not the myths and the fears and the cultural baggage, but the real animal. Plus, he was a visionary who left the state a great gift of Rocky Mountain National Park, and he was a non-conforming, inspired eccentric. How can one not love such a guy?

Standing in his cabin, I looked around: thirteen by thirteen feet, one window, one door, one stove, one table. He was fifteen years old when he came to Estes Park, sixteen when he built the cabin, and twenty-eight when he earned the homestead. He raised two orphan grizzly cubs on this very floor, giving them their first saucers of milk. With this cabin as his home base, he hiked and snowshoed great distances, wrote about bears and geology and wildlife, and worked hard to create a national park that might preserve them. I looked down at the rough floorboards, I looked up at the timbered roof, the log walls, and I looked out the window at the perfectly placed view of Longs Peak, with two pines framing the view—and I thanked Enos Mills for his gift.

Enos Mills has been called the John Muir of the Rockies and the father of Rocky Mountain National Park. He was self-educated, self-made man who started early and lived strong. He became a speaker, a naturalist, a conservationist, an innkeeper, a writer, and he tried his best to change deep-rooted fears about the grizzly, and worked hard to paint a different portrait of an animal that, although it could be provoked into dangerous behavior, was mainly intelligent, curious, and playful. He also did his best—although he ultimately failed—to keep grizzlies alive in Colorado.

Mills was born in Kansas in 1870, and was often too sick with an unspecified illness to work at the family farm. At the age of thirteen, in fact, he was told by a doctor he wouldn't live long. With his parents' blessing—and probably a sense of impending doom—he left home and built this cabin at the foot of Longs Peak, where his health dramatically improved. "After that, he was on the move all the time," his great-granddaughter Eryn Mills told me, as we stood at the door of his cabin. We'd just snowshoed up to his home, through the snow and the hush of a January afternoon, and our warm breath misted out into the cold. "I doubt he stayed here much. There was too much to see." She waved her arm at the view outside, and then stomped her feet to stay warm.

And indeed, move he did. When Mills wasn't leading groups up Longs Peak (he climbed it over 300 times), he was hanging out with grizzly bears or advocating for the creation of a national park in the Rockies near a small village of Estes Park. He was also running a business—after homesteading his cabin and land, he bought Longs Peak Inn, which was right near his cabin, and conducted tours from there. He didn't allow drinking or smoking at the inn—people were there to learn, and he expected them to attend lectures at night and hike in the day. Thousands of tourists came before the national park was even created.

Mills also served the federal government as a consultant on forestry, took snow measurements in the high country for the state of Colorado, and did mail runs to pay bills. It seems to me, in fact, that he mainly worked so that he could be outside, watching grizzlies.

OF ALL THE READINGS I have done on bears, *The Grizzly*, Enos Mills' 1919 book, is my all-time favorite. It's full of accounts of watching grizzlies play in the water, or grizzlies watching river otters play. Grizzlies digging for roots or mice, grizzlies stretching and scratching a tree. He records grizzlies from North Park, Middle Park, South Park, Longs Peak, Grand Lake, the San Juans, and the "No-Summer Mountains" (now called the Never Summers). He covers the ground near my own home, even: "One gray February day, snowshoeing along the Big South Poudre, I chanced to look across an opening... and saw a grizzly walking round and round."

Enos Mills was outside his cultural zeitgeist in more ways than one, but in particular with his disdain for a gun and his preference for being in nature simply to be there. Again and again, he slips in his philosophy: "Generally the gun hampers full enjoyment of the wilderness," he wrote. And in another essay: "The hunter misses most of the beauty and the glory of the trail....Trailing the grizzly without a gun is the very acme of hunting. The gunless hunter...lingers to watch the bear and perhaps her cubs. He sees them play....The information that he gathers and his enjoyment excel those obtained by the man with a gun." In another, he wrote, "The man without a gun can enjoy every scene of nature along his way. He has time to turn aside for other animals, or to stop and watch any one of the countless unexpected wild-life exhibitions that are ever appearing."

That Theodore Roosevelt was hunting for bears in the Colorado mountains at this same time was not lost on Mills—he takes pains to gently contrast those whose outdoor ethic he likes, as opposed to those he doesn't: "Roosevelt has said and shown that the hunter whose chief interest is in the shooting has but little out of the hunt. Audubon [also] did a little shooting for specimens...Thoreau enjoyed life in the wilderness without a gun. But John Muir was the supreme wilderness hunter and wanderer. He never carried a gun...But the wealth of nature-lore with which he enriched his books make him the Shakespeare of nature."

He also argued that the grizzly had been mistakenly represented—basically, that bears were far safer then commonly portrayed. Noting that sensationalist, evil-grizzly stories are "purely fictitious, and, though not even pretending to be fact, appear to have been taken seriously by thousands," he continues to report peaceable grizzlies, who want nothing more than to sleep, eat, dig for grubs, play with cubs. He notes that "it is practically impossible for the average individual to know the real grizzly bear. This comes near to being the immortality of error. It is a national misfortune."

Raised a Quaker, Mills "was against blood sport," Eryn told me. He didn't fish or trap, although he did eat meat—he traded for it. "Since he didn't hunt, he didn't smell like gunpowder. He would just sit and wait. He was patient," Eryn added.

It was not just attitude about game-hunting that Mills was trying to change. At the same time, he was trying to repaint the mental assumptions of grizzlies, and replace the image of horrible-grizzly with something else. "In a grizzly bear we have the leading animal of North America," Mills writes. "He is self-contained and is prepared for anything....He has bulk, agility, strength, endurance, repose, courage, enthusiasm, and curiosity."

One of Mills' most effective ways of rendering the grizzly as something other than evil are his humorous stories. Indeed, Mills has many amusing run-ins with bears, as when he writes, "One of the best play exhibitions that I have ever enjoyed was that of a grizzly juggling with an eight-foot log in a mountain stream." Another time, he recounts a time in which he watching water ouzels, only to realize a bear watching *him*: "I saw a grizzly raised on hind legs with fore paws resting on top of the boulder against which I was leaning."

One of the most captivating stories is that of a hunter who goes on a trip with him and shoots a sow. When they went back to skin her the next day, her cubs were next to her body, whimpering and crying. One cub pawed the body and sat down next to the mother, the other stood "looking into his mother's moveless face...then, all forlorn, he turned to look eagerly into the face of the hunter, who had been watching the little cub all this while with big tears upon his cheeks." They carried the orphans to camp, and the hunter raised them—their mother was the last animal that hunter ever shot, according to Mills.

In *Wild Animal Homesteads*, another of his books, he tells the tale of a cub orphaned by a landslide, wandering around looking for its mother. Another mother grizzly adopts it; and later he sees the mother saving both cubs from a hunter. "The grizzly mother is the greatest wild mother of the wilderness," he writes. "With keen senses and capable brain she ever endeavors to keep her young far from danger...I have not known a mother grizzly to desert her cubs even in the face of hopeless odds."

Cubs, unsurprisingly, seem to be his favorite thing to watch: "It is ever a joy to watch a grizzly and her children. A mother grizzly crossing a lake just south of Long's [sic] Peak swam low in the water with a cub sitting contentedly on her back." Another time he watches a cub give all its attention to the play of mountain sheep.

His love for cubs may have even been responsible for the start of the Denver Zoo. His younger brother Joe (with whom he had a tumultuous relationship) had shot a sow, leaving two orphan cubs. Enos placed them both in a sack and walked them back to his cabin. Here, he gave them a saucer of milk and named them Jenny and Johnny. Later, he had trouble finding good care for them when he traveled, so he gave them to the Denver Zoo ("which was more like a barnyard at that time," Eryn told me). Now they could charge admission—and a zoo was born. Mills seemed troubled by this—both the taking of the cubs, and the gifting of the bears—but underlying his account of it is the quiet hope that they would serve as emissaries to teach others about grizzlies.

For all his admiration, Mills was not overly romantic. He warns that bears could be dangerous, reminding people that the "grizzly objects to being killed." Gently, he tries to explain their behavior: "If he is surprised or crowded so that he sees no escape, if the cubs are in danger or the mother thinks they are... Almost every animal—wild or domestic—will fight if cornered."

Mills, cornered himself, also fought—for his livelihood and life. But before the fighting, was love. Eryn told me the harmonious part: The winter of 1916-1917 had been a gray and long one, and as soon as the clouds broke, a woman named Esther snowshoed from Estes Park to Grand Lake unarmed, by herself, in the moonlight. "No one had done that before," Eryn said. "Enos heard about Esther, and followed her to the general store. Here, she was warned about going out at night—too many bears, to which she replied that she'd like to see one." That was enough to snag the thus-far bachelor Mills; they got married in the doorway of his cabin.

After four years of marriage, one child (a daughter, Edna), and busy days running the Longs Peak Inn, a series of events turned into the hardest battle Mills fought—and eventually lost. Enos Mills witnessed his great goal—Rocky Mountain National Park was created by an Act of Congress in January, 1915 (Mills Lake—a popular destination—is named in his honor). Right after the National Park Service was established, however, they created a monopoly for transportation. Ironically, Mills' own efforts had put him out of work—he could no longer guide in the mountains. He fought hard to change policy and to break the monopoly controlled by the Rocky Mountain Transportation Company, a private company given sole lease to the roads in the park. But then a series of unfortunate events happened. First, in 1921, he had major dental work done, which possibly resulted in an infection. He then went to New York to lobby for his job and was in a subway wreck, where he sustained some sort of spinal injury. He came home, caught the flu, had another tooth surgery (he had an abscess and was probably suffering from sepsis). And during all this, he undoubtedly would have been aware of the steep decline—and near extinction—of grizzlies in northern Colorado. By the 1920s, they were gone. In 1922, Mills died—some say of heartache.

BEFORE LEAVING HIS CABIN, I glanced around one last time. On the walls were various newspapers, old letters, maps. There were a Braille note from Helen Keller, a telegram from Theodore Roosevelt. As we parted, I asked Eryn to leave me with an image of him, and she told me how he had a "crazy, windblown look, with blue eyes. He would get onstage in his suit—people hiked in suits back then—with a high starched collar and knickerbockers with thick wool socks and hob-nail hiking boots."

"Ah," I said, looking at her huge gray-blue eyes, her jeans and hiking boots and flannel shirt. "Got any Enos in you?"

She smiled. "The writing part. And nature too," she said, shrugging. "I'm fond of bears. And when I'm doing my taxes, I'd much rather be hiking!"

One thing that would cheer Enos would be to know his great-granddaughter still lives on his original land; that she sees what he saw; that she appears just as tough and as spirited as I imagine his being. As we snowshoed away, toward Longs Peak, I remembered a particular quotation, one in which Mills seemed caught in a moment of joy. He wrote, "A rugged, snowy peak loomed grim behind the scene, and the dense forest spread away for miles below. The bears, the ptarmigan, and the sheep, the white peak, the purple forest, and the blue sky gave me a striking experience."

After we snowshoed back to my car, Eryn helped me dig out my four-wheel-drive Subaru, laughably stuck in the snow, with a snowshoe. We stood there, panting, smiling, and working until it was free. As I left the mountain, I looked around the wilderness and felt a yearning for grizzlies; simply, I wished they were still out there, making the wildness more wild. And if they were, now I knew that they wouldn't be horrible or as dangerous as I'd once believed—in fact, I was sure I'd be in far more danger pulling out of the driveway onto snowpacked, slick roads. So I made a wish for Enos, if not for the return of the grizzly, then for a real understanding of them. As he gently put it, "It would be a glorious thing if every one appreciated the real character of the grizzly bear."

BEING GOOD
TO BEARS

By Enos Mills

ON THE SLOPE of Long's Peak one June morning I came upon two tiny grizzly bear cubs. Each was about the size of a cottontail rabbit—a lively little ball of fur, dark gray, almost black, in color.

Knowing that their mother had recently been killed, I thought I would capture them and bring them up properly. But they did not want to be brought up properly! We had a lively chase, dodging among the boulders and trees. Cornering them at last among the fallen logs, I grabbed one. He did the same to me. His teeth were as sharp as needles and almost as sharp were his lively claws. It was some time before I could tear myself loose. He kept a mouthful of my trousers. At last I deposited the fighting little fellow in the bottom of a sack. Two grizzly bears in the same sack! Any one should have known better!

I started to conduct them personally to my cabin, two miles away. In descending a steep moraine with the sack over my shoulder I slipped and shook the sack more than any sack should have been shaken that contained two bears. Of course, they started to fight. One bit through the sack and bit the wrong bear. I finally reached my cabin with a long pole over my shoulder. Tied to the south end of the pole was a sack full of grizzly bears.

I shook the cubs out of the sack in front of a basin of milk and thrust their faces deeply into it. Not having eaten for three days, they were "as hungry as bears" and needed no explanation concerning the milk. They had eager, cunning little faces, and were pets before sundown. In twenty-four hours Jenny knew that her name was Jenny, and Johnny that his was Johnny. After a few days they followed me about with fondness and loyalty.

These bears responded to kind treatment and were of cheerful disposition. I made it a point never to annoy or tease them. The grizzly bear is an exceedingly sensitive animal, and annoyances or cruelty make him cross. Once in addressing an audience concerning wild life [sic] I made the statement that bears would be good to us if we were good to them. A small boy instantly asked, "What do you do to be good to bears?" The health and the temper of bears, as well as of people, are easily ruined by improper food.

Young bear cubs are the most wide-awake and observing little people that I know of. Never have I seen a horse or dog who understood as readily or learned as rapidly as these two bears. One day I offered Johnny a saucer of milk. He was impatient to get it. Reaching up, he succeeded in spilling it, but he licked the saucer with satisfaction. On the second try he spilled only a part of the milk. On the third trial he clasped the saucer deftly in his two fore paws [sic], and lifted it upwards, turned his head back and poured the milk into his mouth.

When Johnny and Jenny were growing up, it seemed as if nothing unusual escaped them. A bright button, a flash of a ring, a white handkerchief, or an unusual movement or sound instantly caught their attention. They concentrated on each new object and endeavored to find out what it was.

Having satisfied their curiosity or obtained full information about it, the next instant they were ready to concentrate on something else. But they remembered on second appearance anything which had especially interested them at any time. They learned through careful observation.

For a time they were not chained and had the freedom of the yard. Never have I seen two young animals more intense, more playful, or more energetic. They played alone, they mauled each other by the hour, and occasionally they scrapped. Sometimes we ran foot-races. From a scratch upon the ground, at the word "go," we would race down hill about one hundred and fifty yards. They were eager for these races and always ready to line up with me. They were so speedy that in every race they merrily turned around at least twice to see if I was coming, and in those days I was not slow.

Johnny and Jenny enjoyed playing with people, with any one who did not annoy them. Among the strangers who came was a man who made friends at once and had a good romp. When he left them and went to lunch, Johnny and Jenny followed and lay down near the door where he had disappeared. As he came out, they rose up and started another romp.

To attract my attention or to ask for something to eat, Johnny and Jenny would stand on hind legs and hold out fore paws like an orator. If I came around the corner of the house a quarter of a mile away, they instantly stood on tiptoe and gesticulated with enthusiasm. They were the life of my home, and occasionally almost the death of it.

It was almost impossible to get these cubs filled up. That ate everything—scraps from the table, rhubarb, dandelions, bitter sage, and bark—but they were especially fond of apples. If I approached with meat and honey upon a plate but with apples or turnips in my pockets, they would ignore the plate and, clinching me, thrust their noses into my pockets to find the promised treat.

One August evening I brought in a cluster of wild raspberries for Johnny and Jenny. While still more than a hundred feet from the cabin, both bears leaped to their feet, scented the air, and came racing to meet me with more than their ordinary enthusiasm. No child of frontier parents could have shown more interest in a candy package on the father's return from the city than did Johnny and Jenny in those berries.

A number of people were waiting in my cabin to see me. The little bears and I crowded in. I handed Jenny a berry-laden spray, and then one to Johnny, alternating until they were equally divided. Standing erect, each held the cluster under the left forearm by pressing it against the chest. When browsing in a raspberry-patch bears commonly bit off the tips of the canes together with the leaves and the berries. Johnny and Jenny ate more daintily. One berry was plucked off at a time with two front claws and dropped into the mouth. As one berry followed another, the lips were smacked, and the face and every movement made expressed immense satisfaction at the taste.

Every one [sic] crowded close to watch the performance. In the jostling one of the berry-laden canes fell to the floor. Both little bears grabbed for it at the same instant. They butted heads, lost their temper, and began to fight over it. I grabbed them by the collars and shook them.

"Why, Johnny and Jenny," I said, "why do you do this? And such awful manners when we have company! What shall I do with you?"

They instantly stopped quarreling and even forgot the berries. For several seconds the little bears were embarrassed beyond all measure. They simply stared at the floor. Then suddenly each appeared to have the same idea. Standing erect, facing each other, they put fore paws on each other's shoulders, and went "Ungh, ah, oooo." Plainly they were very sorry that they had misbehaved.

The manner in which these cubs received the berries, the fact that the first time they saw mushrooms they scented them at some distance and raced for them, also that on other occasions they went out of their way to get a plant ordinarily liked by the grizzly, led me to think that they inherited a taste for a number of things that grizzlies commonly eat.

One day we were out walking, when we came upon an army of ants. Without the least hesitation Johnny and Jenny followed along the line, licking them up. Upon reaching the stone behind which the ants were disappearing, Johnny thrust one fore claw under it and flung it aside. I was astonished at his strength.

I tried not to teach Johnny or Jenny any trick, but encouraged them to develop any original stunt or individuality of their own. One day Jenny was attracted by a big green fly that alighted on Johnny. She struck at it; the fly relighted and she struck again. With a little effort I succeeded in getting the bears to shoo flies off each other, and sometimes they were both busy at the same time. It made a comical show, especially when one was lazily lying down and the other was shooing with eagerness and solemnity.

Another activity I encouraged was the bear's habit of holding the other around the neck with one fore paw and rubbing or scratching the back of the bear's head with his other paw. In a short time both bears, while facing each other, would go through the performance at the same time.

Like other children Johnny and Jenny were fond of water and spent much time rolling and wading in the brook by their shed. This was a play they enjoyed. I showed interest in having them roll and splash in the liveliest manner possible.

Johnny seemed unusually interested in what I was doing one day and imitated in succession a number of my performances. I had dropped a penny on the floor, and then, stooping over, touched it with the end of one finger and moved it rapidly about. He rose on his hind feet, held up on claw, then, stooping, put this upon the penny and moved it rapidly about. Blowing the yolk out of an egg, I held up the empty shell before him, and then proceeded to move it rapidly about on the floor with the point of one finger. After licking the shell Johnny imitated my every act without crushing the shell.

While Jenny was asleep on the grass, I placed a large umbrella over her. When she opened her eyes, she at once commenced a quiet though frightened study of the strange thing. She closed one eye, turned her head to one side, and looked up into it; then, turning her head, closed the other eye for a look. A sudden puff of wind gave life to the umbrella and this in turn to Jenny. She made a desperate dash to escape the mysterious monster. The wind whirled the umbrella before her and she landed in it. Wrecking the umbrella, she fled in terror, bellowing with every jump. It took more than an hour to explain matters and assure Jenny that I had not been playing any tricks.

Scotch, my short-nosed collie, was with me when Johnny and Jenny were growing up. Johnny and Scotch were fond of each other, and though each was a little jealous of the master's attention to the other, they got along admirably. Ofttimes they wrestled, and sometimes in their rough and tumble they played pretty roughly. As a climax often Scotch would aim for a neck-hold on Johnny and hammer him on the tip of his sensitive nose with one fore paw, while Johnny if possible would seize Scotch's tail in his mouth and shut down on it with his needle-like teeth.

One of the most interesting pranks which they played on each other was over a bone. Scotch was enjoying this, when he discovered Johnny watching him eagerly. Plainly Johnny wanted that bone. After a little while Scotch leaped to his feet, looked off in the direction beyond Johnny and barked, as though some object of interest was coming from that direction. Then, picking up the bone, he walked away. As he passed in front of Johnny he dropped the bone and gave a bark. Going on a short distance, he barked once or twice more and lay down watching this pretended object in the distance. Johnny was more interested in the bone, but Scotch had dropped this a foot or two beyond his reach, chained as he was. For some time Johnny stood with his nose pointing at the bone, apparently thinking deeply as to how he might reach it. At last, stretching his chain to the utmost he reached out with his right arm. But he could not touch it. Although realizing that he probably could not reach it with the left arm, nevertheless he tried.

All this time Scotch was watching Johnny out of the corner of his eye and plainly enjoyed his failures. Johnny stood looking at the bone; Scotch continued looking at Johnny. Suddenly Johnny had an idea. He wheeled about, reached back with his hind food and knocked the bone forward where he could pick it up with fore paws. Scotch, astonished, leaped to his feet and walked off without a bark or once looking back.

When Johnny and Jenny were small they often reminded me of a little boy and a little girl. Sometimes they would follow me into my cabin. If I sat down they would come close, stand on hind legs, put fore paws on my knees, and look up at me. They would play with my watch-string, peep into my pockets, notice my pencil, or look at the buttons on my coat. Sometimes they would make a round of the room, scrutinize an unusual knot in a log, or stop to look for several seconds at the books in the shelves or the last magazine-cover. Then again, like children, they would walk round the room, tap with their fore paws here and there, and hurry on as children do. More than once they climbed up into my lap, twitched my ears, touched my nose, played with my hair, and finally fell off to sleep, one on each arm.

One day, while I was carrying Johnny in my arms, it occurred to me that he would enjoy a big rocking-chair. I placed him in a chair with one fore paw on each arm. He sat up like a little old man. As I started the chair rocking, he showed his suspicion and alarm by excitedly peering over, first at one rocker and then the other. Presently he calmed down and seemed to enjoy the movement. By and by he caught the swing and rocked himself. Suddenly the little old man and the rocker went over backward. Seeing his angry look as he struck the floor, I leaped upon the centre [sic] table. Getting his feet, he struck a blow that barely missed me and then made lively bites at my ankles. He blamed me for the law of falling bodies. After a few seconds he was as playful as ever, remembering that I had never played any tricks on him, and realizing that I was not to blame for what had happened....

One September we went camping out in Wild Basin, Johnny and Jenny racing along as happy as two boys. Sometimes they were ahead of me, sometimes behind; occasionally they stopped to wrestle and box. At night they lay close to me beside the camp-fire [sic]. Often I used one of them for a pillow, and more than once I awoke to find that they were using me for one.

As we were climbing along the top of a moraine, a black bear and her two cubs came within perhaps thirty feet of us. They saw or scented us. The cubs and their mother bristled up and ran off terribly frightened, while Johnny and Jenny only a short distance in front of me, walked on, but ludicrously pretending that they had not seen the black bears. Surely they were touched with aristocracy!

The man in charge of my place neither understood nor sympathized with wide-awake and aggressive young grizzlies, and once, when I was away, he teased Johnny. The inevitable crash [sic] came and the man went to the hospital. On another occasion he set a pan of sour milk on the ground before Jenny. Bears learn to like sour milk, but Jenny had not learned and she sourly sniffed at it. The man roared, "Drink it," and kicked her in the ribs. Again we had to send for the ambulance.

At last it appeared best to send Johnny and Jenny to the Denver Zoo. Two years went by before I allowed myself the pleasure of visiting them. A number of other bears were with them in a large pen when I leaped in, calling "Hello, Johnny!" as I did so. Johnny jumped up fully awake, stood erect, extended both arms, and gave a few joyful grunts in the way of greeting. Back among the other bears stood Jenny on tiptoe, eagerly looking on.

Excerpted from *The Grizzly: Our Greatest Wild Animal*, by Enos A. Mills. Boston: Houghton Mifflin, 1919.

Fast Grizzly Facts

Ursus arctos horribilis

Description: The grizzly bear is so named because its hair is grizzled, or silver tipped, yet the name is commonly believed to be derived from "grisly," meaning "horrible." A subspecies of brown bear, the grizzly bear is distinguished by its large size and a distinctive hump between the shoulders (this hump is actually a mass of muscle, which enables bears to dig and use their paws as a striking force). Grizzlies range in color from blonde, brown, black, and shades thereof. Adult males typically weigh from 300 to 800 pounds, while females range between 200 and 450 pounds. Some male grizzlies stand eight feet tall on their hind legs.

Habitat: Grizzlies are highly adaptable and flourish in high mountain forests, subalpine meadows, arctic tundra, wetlands, grasslands, mixed-conifer forests, and coastal areas.

Range: Grizzly bears are found today in Alaska, Wyoming, Montana, Idaho, and Washington, as well as in western Canada. Historically, they ranged from Alaska to Mexico and from the Pacific Ocean to the Mississippi River, but their numbers were vastly reduced by western expansion.

Migration: Grizzlies hibernate rather than migrate. Males disperse to set up new territories or reclaim lost habitat; females are presumed to disperse over shorter distances. Grizzlies can travel dozens of miles; territory sizes are thought to be a function of food density.

Breeding: Females reach sexual maturity around five years of age and are considered fully grown at eight to ten years of age. They breed in the late spring and delay implantation of fertilized eggs until November, enabling young to be born during the mother's winter sleep. Cubs remain with their mothers for up to four years, and females won't breed again while in the company of their young. The grizzly bear has one of the slowest reproductive rates of all North American mammals.

Feeding: Grizzly bears are omnivores, feeding on just about anything: insects, berries, nuts, bulbs, roots, carrion, and fish. Salmon is an important food source for grizzlies in Canada and Alaska. Another major food source for some grizzlies is army cutworm moths—during the summer, a grizzly in Yellowstone may consume up to 20,000 army cutworm moths a day. Grizzlies will store found carrion and cover it with grass and moss, which act as a preservative.

Threats: Most threats stem from habitat degradation by land development, logging, road building, oil and gas drilling, livestock grazing, and other resource exploitation. In the Yellowstone region, the whitebark pine nut, which is a primary food source, is in decline due to pine bark beetle infestations.

Populations: Between 1850 and 1970, grizzlies were eliminated from 98 percent of their original range. Populations plummeted from an estimated high of 50,000 to between 800 and 1,200 today. Because of this dramatic decline, their populations in the contiguous U.S. were listed as threatened under the Endangered Species Act in 1975.

Conservation status: The grizzly was listed as a threatened species in the lower 48 U.S. states in 1975 under the Endangered Species Act.

FAST BLACK BEAR FACTS

URSUS AMERICANUS

COLORADO ONCE HAD GRIZZLIES, but officially now has only one type of bear: the American black bear (*Ursus americanus*). There are approximately 10,000 to 12,000 of them in the state and this species is Colorado's largest surviving carnivore.

Description: Black is a species, not a color, and in Colorado many black bears are blonde, black, reddish, cinnamon, or brown. In a Coloradan population, 83 percent of bears of both sexes were brown, not unusual for black bears in mountainous regions of the West. Considerable seasonal color change occurs as a result of bleaching and fading of the pelage. Sub-adults may change color with age, usually going from brown to black. A white chest blaze is not uncommon for Coloradan animals. The muzzle is typically pale brownish yellow. Black bears average three feet tall when standing on all for feet. Males average 275 pounds and females 175 pounds.

Habitat: Montane shrublands and forests, and subalpine forests at moderate elevations.

Diet: Over 90 percent of a black bear's diet is grasses, berries, fruits, nuts, and plants. The rest is primarily insects and scavenged carcasses. Bears are omnivorous and the diet depends largely on what kinds of food are seasonally available, although their mainstay is vegetation. In spring, emerging grasses and succulent forbs are favored. In summer and early fall, bears eat a variety of berries and other fruits. In late fall, preferences are for berries and mast (acorns), where available. Black bears will also eat a diversity of insects, including beetle larvae and social insects (ants, wasps, bees, termites, etc.), and they kill a variety of mammals, including rodents, rabbits, and young or unwary ungulates.

Life span: 20-25 years in the wild.

Attributes: Black bears hibernate around early November and emerge from dens around early May. On average, two cubs are born in the den in late January. Bears aren't naturally nocturnal, but sometimes travel at night in hopes of avoiding humans.

Range in Colorado: Black bears are locally common in suitable habitats in the western two-thirds of the state. The highest population densities occur in the montane shrublands from Walsenburg and Trinidad west to the San Luis Valley, in the San Juan Mountains, and in the canyon country of west-central Colorado.

CRAWLING INTO THE DEN

BEAR DENS smell good. I know because I've been in one, face up against a bear—head-first, flat-on-my-stomach, in a narrow rocky outcropping. I was drenched in sweat, huffing, and thinking, *Isn't it supposed to stink in here?* and *I have never been happier.*

But my happiness was irrelevant. It was the bears' well-being that was germane, which is why eleven of us snowshoed up 1200 feet on a mountainside near the town of Aspen—a trip that involved several hours of grunting, whispering, cussing the undergrowth, cussing the "rotten" snow, and, in my case, taking off my snowshoes in order to re-tie my boots, promptly sinking to my waist, only to crawl out and sink again. On this trip were several researchers from Colorado State University, two veterinarians, and a couple of Colorado Parks and Wildlife folks. They were all carrying heavy backpacks laden with heavy equipment—tranquilizer guns, medical equipment, avalanche shovels, antennas for receiving signals. There were also a couple of onlookers, such as myself, carrying snacks and water and those sticky heat-patch things, and the burden of naiveté and the buoyant respect that accompanies traveling with people who know their stuff.

The experts among us had located this den with two hibernating black bears—a sow and her yearling—and had dug out the den and tranquilized the two bears (with the utmost care and grace and gentleness). They had covered the sow's face with a soft hat, in order to protect her face from getting scratched up, and had pulled her out to the rocky outcropping. Since there wasn't room for both bears on the ledge, the yearling was left inside the den. Which is how I found myself lying with the mother bear behind me and the yearling in front of me—freezing cold and sandwiched between two good-smelling examples of *Ursus americanus*.

LET SLEEPING BEARS LIE. Or, in other words, why *do* this—snowshoe up a very steep, very remote slope on a freezing cold day to bother hibernating black bears? To help the bears. Or, to be more specific, to help humans know how to live with bears, which ultimately helps us both.

After I'd been pulled backwards, out of the den, by my feet (by scientists and graduate students, in what was a somewhat embarrassing maneuver for me), I stood with Colorado Parks and Wildlife (CPW) District Wildlife Manager Kevin Wright, who stomped his feet, pulled on his gloves, and taught me about Colorado's bears: black bears are native; there are approximately 10,000 to 12,000 in the state; they are many colors ranging from black to blonde; they've got a sense of smell that is 100 times better than people's; and they've lost much of their habitat as human population increases. Bear-human conflicts are sharply on the rise, accounting for about one-third of all bear deaths in the state.

Aspen, in fact, might well be the epicenter of conflicts—Wright noted that in 2009, CPW handled over 900 calls, and Kevin euthanized 21 bears, and relocated over 30. "Man, I *hate* putting down bears," he said, as we stood gazing at the scientists working over the bear. "I *hate* it," and although it's possible that the ice-balls hanging from his beard and clothes caused his eyes to water, it's also possible that what I saw was a sudden flush of tears.

I jogged in place and swung my arms around, nearly crying myself from the cold. "What would help?"

Three basic things, he said, would solve about 95 percent of bear-human conflicts: bear-proofing garbage, locking doors at night, and closing accessible windows. "It's so simple," he added. "People need to take responsibility for where they choose to live."

"It seems pretty common sense," I said.

"Yes," he said, "not rocket science."

But the science of what to do with "nuisance bears" was exactly why we'd all snowshoed up here in the first place. The researchers, in fact, have been able to partially dispel the notion that "a fed bear is a dead bear." Most bears near this mountain town do *not* become habituated to human food sources as much as we think they do—they will go back to natural food as soon as those food sources are available. In other words, fed bears don't necessarily become dependent on human food sources. Yes, bears are opportunists, but take away the "opportune" part and they won't be "ists." Two graduate students at Colorado State University, Sharon Baruch-Mordo and David Lewis (who was leading on this trip, breaking trail the entire way), have been conducting studies that illustrate that bears exhibit "behavior plasticity," a fancy way of saying that bears have the ability to change their habits. Bears, they note, will return to their preferred Colorado diet of chokecherries, gamble oak, and serviceberry—the three main mass producing berries for bears in Colorado—once those foods are available. This feels like huge news to me, because it calls into question the idea of bears becoming "ruined."

SPEED AND GRACE. That could probably apply to bears, but since the bears were knocked out, I was marveling at the team's quick and sure work with the bears. Julie Mao, a CPW biologist, and Lisa Wolfe, a CPW veterinarian, squatted over the bear, holding unused blood vials in their mouths, eyes closed in concentration as they felt for a vein and then drew blood. They administered eye drops and ointments and muttered vet-like information to each other. David Lewis and Kevin Wright were also fast at work: the bear was covered with a space blanket, measurements were taken, fragments of whispered conversation floated in the air: "considering the girth, I'm guessing 177 pounds," and "seven years old," and "three cubs last year" and "dart in at 1:15."

But mostly, as I huddled against a rock outcropping, I forgot about the humans and studied the bear—her feet pads (so soft) and teeth (so yellow) and fur (so predictably but surprisingly thick). I rejoiced when her heavy-looking radio collar was cut off—it was no longer needed since the study in this area being concluded—she simply looked more comfortable without it.

Tranquilizers don't last forever, and as the humans hurried to finish up as the mama started huffing, the bears were given a shot of antibiotics ("Hey, give that shot in a few places, it will sting her less," Kevin instructed, which prompted a woman to lean over and whisper to me, "That guy loves bears," and another to murmur, "Yeah, he's such a softie"). With a lot of care, the bear was put back into her den, next to her yearling, the opening was covered, and the bears left in solitude once more.

As we quietly picked up our gear and prepared to leave, I regarded the bear claw marks on the aspen trees. I've seen bear-scars before, arcs of five claws in beautiful patterns, healed over by the aspen—but these trees were tremendous, scarred nearly from top to bottom, as if the whole tree was a bear's canvas. These aspens will be among the first things the bears feed on; the first blooms, called aspen catkins, are what will help coax the bear awake.

On the way back down the mountain, some of the team telemarked down, some slid on their avalanche shovels. I klutzily half-snowshoed, half-slid down the steep mountainside in a reckless uncoordinated way, past the aspen trees and pines and down into meadow. Once at the bottom, I straightened up, caught my breath, brushed off the snow frozen to my clothes, realized I had bruises forming on my derriere, and promised myself a hot bath at the first random hotel I came to. Then I looked back up in the direction of the den.

There are a lot of bear myths out there, and this trip dispelled some for me. Bears do not hibernate in big roomy caves, but rather under fallen trees or in rocky outcroppings; bears do not defecate or urinate while hibernating (hence the good smell); bears are not really asleep when hibernating and can come at you at thirty-five miles per hour (as opposed to humans, who would atrophy after sleeping so much); bears make great huffing noises; and, it is better to tranquilize a bear in the shoulder than the butt. But most importantly, I was reminded of the fact that bears don't want to have much to do with humans, and with a little work on our part, we can keep them wild.

FIRM IN THE FAITH OF THE WILDERNESS

THE DEATH OF COLIN MCCLELLAND

COLIN MCCLELLAND was only twenty-four—tall and blond and thin, he was a young man who was still filling out and growing up. He had big plans ahead of him, and an enormous amount of outdoor experience behind him. A quiet person, he loved the outdoors and had found a way to make a living there—preparing trees for logging on Waugh Mountain, north of Cotopaxi, in the southern part of Colorado. But on August 13, 1993, Colin's body was discovered. He had been killed and partially eaten by a black bear.

As I stood above his grave on a windy day on the outskirts of Buena Vista, I scanned the panoramic view of my favorite range in Colorado. There had just been a spring snowstorm and the Collegiate Peaks were covered in white. I put a small rock on his tombstone, where his father had inscribed the quotation by the famous climber Willie Umsole: FIRM IN THE FAITH OF THE WILDERNESS.

WILDERNESS SEEMED to be the guiding star of this family. Or so it seemed to me, after talking to Colin's father, Al McClelland. That Al had been licensed as an outfitter for thirteen years was just the beginning. He had also started Rocky Mountain Expeditions, the first rafting company in Colorado. He was the first to get winter cross-country skiing permits in the backcountry of the Grand Canyon, where he'd cross-country ski into the north rim with a group in winter gear, change to summer clothes for the hike down, and then put the winter gear back on for the cross-country ski out. He oversaw long expeditions across the Continental Divide, with no food and no tents. His stories of time spent in the backcountry felt as expansive as the mountains themselves—and as varied, too: "I'm a life member of The Sierra Club," he told me. "But I am no liberal tree hugger."

Colin was the recipient of this outdoor knowledge, and was as comfortable in the outdoors as his father. He cross-country skied, hiked, camped, and valued his independence and freedom. It's no surprise, then, that when an outdoor job came his way, he took it. "He found out that the Forest Service was issuing permits to help clear the forest," Al said. "Colin would prepare the trees, and also had an opportunity to sell the aspens, and in so doing, he was making a sizeable amount of money. He didn't want to mess with a tent; he had a trailer."

Here was the problem. At the site of his trailer, which he used as a base for cutting downed lodgepole-pines, he'd had problems with bears for several years. A year before the fatal attack, in fact, a bear had broken into the kitchen and eaten food. Apparently the problem with bears was so bad that he'd taken to sleeping on top of the trailer on some nights. Just two nights before his death, some friends loaned Colin a rifle. "This particular scenario—well, I believe that's what created the problem for the bears," Al told me. "They had someone living in their habitat, and I've been led to believe that there was trash at his campsite that was hauled out periodically by his mother. This bear...well, this bear did what bears do."

It also appears that Colin was ill with a cold—he had taken

some cold medicine (officials did a blood test at the request of Al, and there were no illegal drugs in Colin's system). "I think he was sleeping deeply because of that medication," Al said. "He did manage to get one shot off. But the bear killed him, drug him out of the trailer and buried him in brush nearby. Not a whole lot of him was left to bury because the bear had eaten most of him," Al said in a voice imbued with sorrow.

Two days later, wildlife officers trapped and killed a bear outside the trailer. Human remains were found in its digestive system. The bear apparently fed upon Colin's body two or three times over the course of five to seven days.

"I did go up to the site. With friends. They didn't want me to go in the trailer." Here, Al paused to regain his composure. "And I'm so happy I didn't."

THERE ARE NO teddy bears in the McClelland household. "No one gives anyone a teddy bear," Al told me. "It's just understood. Bears are not like Smokey the Bear or Disneyland. They're something else entirely. This family knows that."

Despite the fact that a bear killed his son, Al doesn't harbor any ill will for the animals. "Regardless of where you are, if you occupy or modify an animal's habitat, there will be a price you need to pay," he told me. "If you build a house in Africa in the natural habitat of elephants, you shouldn't be irritated when elephants come walking through. In Colorado, people build subdivisions around the mountain, and then they get upset about deer. It's not any different. People tend to blame the bears, but it's not the bears. It's the humans and their living habits that create the problem."

In fact, Al is convinced that the vast majority of bears are quiet creatures who want nothing more than to be left alone. Despite thousands of hours spent outdoors, the McClelland family had never had a bit of trouble with them. "The experience we have had is that bears simply do not want to be around you," he said. "Make a noise and they are *gone*. Just like beaver or elk. Given enough time and noise, they'll go. We understand all of that. We've never, ever had a bear bother us. So: how did this bear feel comfortable enough to do what it did? The answer to that is that I am convinced that this was a bear that had been removed from a site—a renegade bear, they're called—and he had been relocated. Where do I come up with that? Because I had someone confide in me that that's where the bear came from."

It's likely no one will know for sure, but Al knows that what transpired was highly unusual. The black bears of Colorado are not, in general, dangerous. "I don't believe the answer is killing bears," he said. "I think the answer is limiting development." He suggested a moratorium on subdivisions and building permits until an environmental impact statement could determine how these stressors affect wildlife such as bears. And in the meantime, people need to live in—and appreciate—the wilderness that they're lucky enough to have.

WHEREVER THE BEAR came from, and whatever happened, there's no doubt that this was a tragedy. But when Al told me there was a silver lining, I shook my head in wonder and disbelief. What good could come from such a sad story?

"Oh, it's true," Al said. "Colin was in an estranged situation with his wife. And they had an infant daughter. During this period, it was agreed by both he and his wife that my wife and I would take custody of their daughter while they were working out their domestic plan. The agreement was that they would not return the child to either parent without both of them agreeing on it. Then my son was killed by a bear. So there was no one to agree. In the end, I adopted my granddaughter. I raised her from the time she was fourteen months old. Now she's married, and doing just fine. More than fine. She's a beautiful young lady, very smart, and at one time was the number two *world* champion in tai kwon do for her age group. And…she's pregnant!"

"It sounds like Colin would be proud," I said.

"Yes. I think the last time I saw him he was in Buena Vista, where he reassured me that he thought his daughter was in best hands." Here, he paused. "I've buried my son and moved on. The fact is, my only born son died. And that's a tragedy. But I think he would be proud, yes."

As I stood above Colin's gravestone and considered the mountains in front of me—a sweeping stunning view—I thought of the quotation that Al left me with. It's a quote, he said, that guides him. It's one from Johann Wolfgang Von Goethe: "Whatever you can do, or dream you can, begin it. Boldness has genius, power, and magic in it."

THE THIN LINE

TRAGIC AND NEAR TRAGIC ENCOUNTERS WITH BLACK BEARS

THERE'S OFTEN a very thin line between life and death. Patrick Finan and Tim Schuett know this too well, and in their case, the line is perhaps as thin as the fabric of their tents.

In 2003, Finan, Schuett, and a group of friends were camped at Rocky Mountain National Park near Fern Lake—a hodgepodge group of a few close friends and a few acquaintances out to enjoy the mountains of Colorado. Only these two men had significant backcountry experience, the rest had little camping experience at all. But they were diligent—Finan told me that the group arrived at Fern Lake, about four miles back from trailhead, set up camp, and took all the usual precautions. They suspended their cooking utensils and removed food and trash from their campsite.

Finan, who had graduated from Duke the year before and was working in a research lab at the psychology department at the University of Colorado in Boulder, was (and still is, according to his wife, he joked) a very deep sleeper. "At about 7:30 in the morning, I woke up in the midst of a dream, and felt an incredible smash in my head—it felt like a baseball bat," he said. "I think I incorporated in my dream some way, and I remember muttering something, and I went back to sleep. Then felt another blow to my head, and that one was so severe I woke up and sat up. Immediately, I saw blood squirting out of my head, spraying everywhere in the tent, blood puddling in my lap."

Finan remembered being confused, trying to figure out what had happened, and seeing a bear—all at the same time. He'd been sleeping with no fly on his tent, and so there was just the thin fabric between him and what he soon discovered was a bear: "I saw the bear standing outside the tent, looking directly in at me. We made eye contact for a second. Then I looked away. I was in a completely helpless position inside my tent—I couldn't hit the bear on the snout or anything. There were a couple of tense seconds there. I don't know how long the bear stood there."

When the bear ambled off, the danger wasn't over. Finan started yelling to wake the other campers, but meanwhile watched as the bear wandered past the tent full of newbie-campers, and directly to a tent occupied by Tim Schuett. Finan saw the bear swipe the outside of the tent, then swipe his tent again. No damage was done to the tent, and so Finan was hopeful (even as he was yelling) that no one inside was injured: "But then I saw the bear walk away, and I saw Tim emerge from tent with blood streaming down his face." He paused. "The tent was just fine. That's a pretty good ad for the tent manufacturer."

Joking aside, the situation was serious. Finan reported that he took shirt off and put it around his head. "I put a good bit of pressure on the wounds. I hadn't been in that situation before, but instinct basically just kicked in," he told me. He didn't know until the rangers got there that he had been bitten both times: "I had multiple puncture wounds. There were very clear marks on my forehead. The bear had put its bottom jaw into the crown into my head, and top sunk into my forehead."

Schuett, too, felt the real possibility of death and the real powers of instinct. "We were up late, and I was sleeping when I felt this intense pressure on my face," he told me. His first impression was that it was a friend messing with him, and "it took a few seconds to realize it was not a nightmare or a friend—that whatever it was had very long claws." The bear swiped the tent again, and that's when Schuett sustained the worst of his injuries—the bear tore his scalp across the top of the head from ear to ear. "As the blood was dripping into my eyes and down my neck, I looked out the mesh of my tent at a pretty big bear. I grabbed the walls of my tent and started screaming," he said. "The bear didn't take off running, but it sort of lost interest and sniffed around and wandered off to a bush. I grabbed a shirt and wrapped it around my head and got out. First, I looked over to my left, and there's Patrick, holding his forehead, and there's four fountains of blood squirting out of his head. That was pure terror. The others were stepping out of their tent, and I could see one guy look at Patrick, then me, and he's as white as a sheet, and then I realized he was looking past me, and there's the bear, foraging in this bush. I turned to look at the bear too, and we made eye contact and then it walked off into the woods. If we had made the wrong choice right then or right after...well, I count myself as extremely fortunate."

What happened next was just as decisive in terms of saving their lives. Schuett told me, "Patrick and I were sitting on a log, the bear had left, and I don't know how to describe it, but a light went on, but I knew my chances of survival were diminishing; I had to take decisive steps to get out of there. We didn't know if the bear would come back, we didn't know anything. We had unevaluated head trauma. We were both quiet; Patrick's wounds were much more visible, and I had a twelve-inch laceration from ear to ear, and

I easily could have bled out if I hadn't had longer hair that staunched the blood."

Luckily, Schuett, like Finan, had outdoor experience—he had, in fact, recently completed a semester at the National Outdoor Leadership School. He said, "I asked Patrick some questions, to see if he had any cerebral damage, and he was able to answer, so I knew he was stable. I was hoping the puncture wounds didn't go through his skull, that he was ambulatory. But I knew we had to get out there as soon as we could. We also had to let other people know."

The group moved down to the lake and sat on a large boulder, where they warned a few dayhikers and a Boy Scout troop. They were also able to get better first aid supplies. Another camper in their group used a cell phone to call for help, and by about ten o'clock, two rangers came up to dress the wounds. Paramedics met them at the trailhead. The group was able to seek medical attention in the nearby town of Estes Park. Finan needed about twenty-five stitches and a rabies vaccination; Schuett had been slashed to the skull and needed about thirty staples.

Both have returned to the wilderness, and neither harbors ill will for bears. "I've been wilderness-camping a fair amount since then," Finan told me. "Bears deserve respect. I don't feel any animosity toward them. I think about bears the way I think about any animal in the wild, which is that we should minimize the impact that we have in all aspects of the wilderness." Schuett agreed, noting that he moved to Colorado after the attack (although he is now a physics teacher in the Chicago suburbs). "Camping is still one of my favorite things to do." He's gone back to Fern Lake a couple of times, telling me that there are "still some bloodstains on the railroad ties." He noted that "part of the price you pay for admission is that you're entering an environment where you are totally not in control. The first time I learned that lesson, I was struck by lightning crossing the Continental Divide" (he was struck by lightning and attacked by the bear in the same year).

As it turned out, though, any amount of preparation or proper bear precaution might not have prevented this particular encounter. Finan explained, "This particular bear, which was killed a few weeks later—it was bluff-charging people on the same trail—had a necropsy done on it. It's my understanding that the bear had some lesions on its brain. This bear was an anomaly. This bear was dis-inhibited because of brain pathology." Schuett added that it's his understanding that mayonnaise packets and tinfoil were found in the bear's gullet.

Does either man worry now? Not particularly. "I'm certainly more vigilant now than before," Finan said. "I take a leadership role in making sure the camp is clean. But our camp was as clean as you would want." In addition, he prefers to stay away from car camping or highly used areas. "It riffles me when I go to Yellowstone and you see how close people get to serious wildlife. There's little way to manage that in a park like that. I prefer to be as remote as possible, where campers can participate in the wilderness without necessarily imposing our will on it."

FINAN AND SCHUETT'S STORY is an anomaly. In fact, more than 21,000 people camp annually in Rocky Mountain National Park, and given those numbers, it strikes me how few bear incidents the park has had. Just two bears have been relocated in the past two years because they were nuisances—and only one person has ever been killed by a bear in Rocky Mountain National Park. In 1971, John Richardson was 31 and a newlywed on his honeymoon when he was dragged out of his tent and killed by an older male black bear. The following day, officials tracked down and killed the animal, and they found it had abscessed teeth and a plastic bucket in its stomach, indicating that it was probably desperate for food.

The only other death caused by black bear in Colorado, according to the Parks and Wildlife, which started tracking bear-human encounters in the 1960s, was that of Donna Munson. She was seventy-four, and lived in the mountains in a cabin north of Ouray. That she loved animals is obvious—she had four dogs and thirty cats and cared for a variety of wildlife, including a sick deer and a skunk. But her relationship with wildlife—an unhealthy one, many would argue—was the very thing that killed her.

In August of 2009, a housekeeper found the partially eaten body of Munson outside her home. Authorities determined that Munson was killed by a black bear, and autopsy results show that she quickly bled to death from slashes to her neck and face.

The problem had been ongoing: The Parks and Wildlife tried to deter Munson, whom officers suspected of feeding bears for decades. According to officials, she had been repeatedly warned by officials to stop. As reported in the *Denver Post*, CPW officials said they had tried to contact Munson about bear-feeding allegations in 2004, 2005 and 2007 before sending a certified letter in April 2008.

Authorities believe Munson was standing on her porch, behind a seven-foot-high wire fence she had built on the property, at the time of the attack. Munson appeared to have been dragged underneath the fence.

PATRICK FINAN and Tim Schuett could have come close to dying; John Richardson, Colin McClelland, and Donna Munson share the unfortunate link of being the three Coloradoans to die because of black bears. In McClelland's and Munson's cases, the deaths very likely could have been prevented—food was a culprit. John Richardson's case seems much like

Finan and Schuett's case—simply a very rare case of being in the wrong place at the wrong time.

The chances of that are slim, but knowing what to do is always empowering. Tom Beck, Colorado's original black bear biologist, suggests the following: First, locate all "exits" for the bear—as in, determine how and where the bear will go to get away from you. Then, don't go there—leave the obvious exits for the bear to take. Stand upright and talk to the bear in a normal voice level; slowly back away from the bear but do not back yourself up against a cliff or tree if you can avoid it. Drop a hat, daypack, or water bottle (anything to distract the bear) on the ground, giving the bear something to investigate while you back away. Meanwhile, don't take your eyes off the bear. Do not run and do not climb a tree—black bears are better climbers than humans and, even worse, climbing may elicit normal aggressive bear responses. Bears will often signify their unease (remember, they are probably stressed out too) by "vocalizing"—huffing and snorting. In nearly all cases, bears will take off through the brush. But in cases when bears have become habituated to humans, they will be more unpredictable. So, while backing away, look for possible weapons—a stick or rock—just in case the bear does charge. Beck concluded by adding, "Remember, stay calm and think. I know this is difficult, but it's the same advice I give myself while driving in Denver."

INDEED, SCHUETT is hopeful that any others who find themselves in his position will end up walking away. "I guess I'm thankful it was me, because I was capable of handling that," he said. "It could have been a much worse turnout—a family with kids, for instance. I don't necessarily believe in fate, but we were placed there, instead of someone else. And we could cope with it." Then he paused and added, "And this whole thing has given me a healthier perspective on life, makes me thankful for every day that I have on this planet."

REPORTED COLORADO BEAR ATTACKS ON HUMANS

1960 TO OCTOBER 2011

EVENTS BETWEEN humans and bears are rare, but conflicts do happen. This list of documented bear attacks was compiled by Colorado Parks and Wildlife and is reprinted with permission. In these reports, "GMU" stands for Game Management Unit, a geographic unit designated by CPW, where GMU maps are available. "Co." stands for County.

Fatal Bear Attacks

July 25, 1971: (Black Bear, GMU 18, Grand Co.) A honeymooning couple was tent camping near Grand Lake. A large older bear entered the tent, injured the woman and pulled the 31-year-old man away from the campsite. The man was killed. The bear was later found and destroyed. Further examination of the black bear found that it had worn, abscessed teeth and a plastic bucket in its stomach. *(Editor's note: See the chapter "The Thin Line.")*

August 10, 1993: (Black Bear, GMU 58, Fremont Co.) A male bear broke into a camper 20 miles north of Cotopaxi, presumably in search for food. The bear killed the 24-year-old male occupant of the trailer. The man was from Buena Vista. The camper tried to deter attack by shooting at the bear. The bear was injured by a bullet that grazed its rib cage, possibly increasing the voraciousness of the attack. A 250-pound, very aggressive male black bear with a fresh bullet wound to the rib cage was trapped and destroyed six days later. A necropsy on the bear revealed human remains in its digestive system. *(Editor's note: See the chapter "Firm in the Faith of the Wilderness.")*

August 7, 2009: (Black Bear, GMU 65, Ouray Co.) A visitor to a home outside of Ouray found the body of the 74-year-old female homeowner, who had been killed and partially eaten by a bear or bears. As sheriff's deputies were investigating the scene, they were approached by a 250-pound, 5-year-old male black bear that exhibited aggressive behavior. Deputies shot and killed the bear after it showed no fear of people. Results of the necropsy on that bear were inconclusive as to whether it was involved in the original incident. Early the next morning, personnel from Wildlife Services killed a 394-pound, mature male black bear that approached the home and exhibited aggressive behavior. A necropsy on the large older boar revealed human remains and remnants of clothing in its digestive system. An autopsy on the victim showed that she bled to death quickly from deep slashes to her head and neck and was likely unconscious due to an initial blow to the head from a bear. The homeowner had constructed a metal fence that covered her porch so that she could feed bears through the fence. In the days leading up to the attack the woman told her family that she was trying to help a smaller bear that had suffered broken teeth in a fight with an older bear. Wildlife officers visited the home dozens of times in previous years to investigate reported feeding, but officers were met with no cooperation. In early July 2009, a caretaker at the residence, concerned about safety, asked wildlife officers to place traps on the property to address problems with aggressive bears. On the first day that traps were placed, two bears were trapped and euthanized. *(Editor's note: See the chapter "The Thin Line.")*

Injuries from Bear Attacks

June, 1966: (Black Bear, GMU 81, Conejos Co.) A black bear pulled a 4-year-old La Jara boy from his sleeping bag while the boy's family was on a cattle drive southwest of Antonito. The boy's 18-year-old brother yelled and threw rocks at the bear, which dropped the boy and fled. The boy required 22 stitches in his neck and head.

September 23, 1979: (Grizzly Bear, GMU 78, Archuleta Co.) An adult sow grizzly was wounded by an archery hunter and then attacked an outfitter. The bear was killed by the outfitter and the hide is at the museum of Natural History in Denver, of the last confirmed grizzly in Colorado. Before killing the bear, the outfitter sustained major but non-life-threatening injuries. He was treated and released from a local hospital.

May 1986: (Black Bear, GMU 75, La Plata Co.) A black bear grabbed a 7-year-old California girl who was with a group of girls sleeping outside near Durango. When the girl screamed, the bear dropped her and retreated. The bear returned and tried to drag off the girl's 11-year-old sister in her sleeping bag. The girl screamed and the bear dropped her and fled. Both girls survived. The 11-year-old was treated for injuries from a bite wound to the head.

May 6, 1989: (Black Bear, GMU 85, Las Animas Co.) A 37-year-old man hunting bears approximately 10 miles west of Aguilar was attacked by the male black bear he had earlier shot and wounded. The hunter and his 15-year-old son saw the bear go down but as they approached, the bear rushed the hunters and pinned the man against a rock. The son shot at the bear to save his father but the bullet struck his father in the upper right chest instead. The elder hunter died from the bullet wound. The bear, a 7-year-old, 307-pound boar, was found dead a mile from the incident and taken to CSU for necropsy.

August 15, 1989: (Black Bear, GMU 38, Jefferson Co.) A 255-pound black bear destroyed the tent of a 36-year-old mother and her 9-year-old daughter. Woman was bitten or clawed on the back of her head, leaving a wound that required 15 stitches. Food had been kept inside the tent. Three Denver SWAT officers found the animal after the attack and shot it.

July 19, 1990: (Black Bear) Yearling black bear weighing approximately 60 pounds attacked a 16-year-old Fruita girl. She received superficial bite wounds on her back. It was later determined that she and other campers had been feeding the bear.

July 18, 1992: (Black Bear, GMU 85, Las Animas Co.) At approximately 3:30 A.M. a man heard something walking outside his tent. As the man was reaching for his shoes to investigate the noise, a black bear came through the side of the tent. The bear grabbed the man by the arm and began to drag him away from the camp. The bear stood on his hind legs with the man's arm in its mouth and raked the man across the back leaving large welts. The man punched the bear in the face with his fist and the bear dropped him and left the site. The man may have brushed/moved the side of the tent when he was reaching for his shoes and precipitated a predatory response in the bear. Pictures of the campsite show an overturned trash can within yards of the tent. There was no food in the tent. The man received 25 stitches at a local hospital.

June 20, 1994: (Black Bear, GMU 85, Las Animas Co.) At approximately 3 A.M., two 14-year-old boys from Texas were awakened when two bears collapsed their tent. One of the boys was scratched and bruised while the other sustained deep puncture wounds and abrasions from being bitten through the tent fabric. The bears also damaged a tent camper and another tent during the attack, but no one else was injured. There was no food in the tent or in the vicinity of the tent. The attack appeared to be unprovoked but interviews indicated one of the boys had reached down to pull a blanket over him immediately before the attack and may have brushed the side of the tent, which has been reported to possibly trigger a predatory response in bears (reaction to movement). It appeared to be a boar and sow involved in the incident. The sow was destroyed when she returned to the scene at daylight. The boar was tracked with dogs most of that day but was not found.

May 17, 1998 (Black Bear, GMU 110, El Paso Co.) A female black bear with dependent cubs confronted a male hiker from Colorado Springs above Garden of the Gods. Victim climbed a tree to escape injury, but sustained puncture wounds on his hip and scratches on his arm. The bear retreated and the man was able to leave the area.

September 18, 1998 (Black Bear, Lake Co.) While attempting to hang a skinned elk from a tree, a 53-year-old male hunter from Greeley was attacked by a 250-pound, female black bear who had fed on the elk carcass the previous night. Victim scaled the tree and was bit in the foot. His hunting partners, one of which was a wildlife officer, chased away the bear and subsequently killed it because of its continued aggressive behavior.

August 4, 1999 (Black Bear, GMU 82, Saguache Co.) A 56-year-old hiker from South Fork surprised a sow black bear and cubs in the Sangre de Cristo Mountains in the northeastern part of the San Luis Valley. The mother bear charged and treed the man. He sustained puncture wounds and scratch marks to his foot, ankle and leg. The bears left the area after making several charges up the tree.

September 13, 2000 (Black Bear, GMU 421, Mesa Co.) A large black bear on Grand Mesa confronted four hunters. One muzzleloader hunter was bitten in the buttocks while on the ground. One bow hunter was knocked down by the bear and bitten on the hand and leg. A third hunter fired three shots with a pistol at the bear; it is believed that only the last shot hit the boar. A few days later that bear was found dead a short distance from the attack site. The 300-pound, 6- or 7-year-old male black bear appeared to have died from a bullet wound to the abdomen.

July 8, 2001 (Black Bear, GMU 85, Huerfano Co.) A 16-year-old Colorado Springs teenager suffered minor injuries when a black bear bit him as he slept in his sleeping bag at a campsite west of Gardner. The boy's uncle killed the 130-pound, 3-year-old male black bear after it returned to the campsite and chased the boy's father onto the top of a pickup truck. Wildlife officers said that the bear had become accustomed to finding human food in the area and made regular visits to the campsite.

July 24, 2001 (Black Bear, GMU 86, Chaffee Co.) A Texas scout leader was bitten and scratched by a black bear that entered her tent while she slept. The bear entered the tent in the early morning hours and was chased off by other scout leaders who responded when the victim yelled for help. On Aug. 1, a 175-pound, 3-year-old, male black bear, which was habituated to human food, was trapped at the campground and destroyed.

August 2, 2001 (Black Bear, GMU 86, Chaffee Co.) A 17-year-old Boy Scout from Kansas suffered a bruised back and other minor injuries early in the morning when a black bear entered his tent in the Packerd High Adventure Scout Camp south of Poncha Springs. The bear was chased off by scout leaders who responded when the victim yelled for help. The victim was sleeping in the exact same tent as the July 24 victim. Wildlife officers noted that the camp did not have bearproof trash containers. Officers closed the campground for the rest of the season. Officers trapped and destroyed a large 295-pound, male black bear on Aug. 6 at the camp.

August 21, 2001 (Black Bear, GMU 86, Fremont-Custer Co. line). In the Lake Creek Campground, a 21-year-old camper from Kansas was awakened just after midnight by a 280-pound male black bear that tore through the side of his tent. The victim told wildlife officials that he was sleeping in a tent with two other people when the bear attacked. He woke up with the bear standing on top of him. He kicked the animal. The bear bit his hand, and the man grabbed a hatchet and began swinging at the animal, initiating a scuffle that lasted 20- 30 seconds. In addition to the bite to his right hand, the man also received injuries to his head, back, and upper right arm. Wildlife officers, using dogs provided by a local hunting outfitter, tracked and destroyed the bear about 7 A.M. Even though the Lake Creek Campground had bear-proof containers and there was no trash lying around, it was closed for the season after the incident. A neighboring private campground also had bear-proof containers but the containers were not closed properly and trash was scattered.

August 27, 2001 (Black Bear, GMU 371, Summit Co.) A 41-year-old California woman sleeping in her tent just north of Frisco suffered a cut early in the morning when a black bear swiped through the tent fabric with its paw. About 6 A.M. the woman felt the muzzle of an animal nudging the side of her tent. She pushed at the muzzle thinking it might be a loose dog and the bear responded by swiping through the fabric with its claws. The woman was cut on the forehead. She yelled and the bear backed off. The woman got out of her tent at the opposite end from where the bear had been. She and the bear looked at each other from about 10 feet away. She told the bear to "go away." The animal left the area and the woman walked down the trail to request help from people in a nearby trailer. After the women left, the bear returned and tore apart the campsite, including the woman's tent and sleeping bag. The campsite was reasonably clean, but there were other informal campsites in the area where food was left lying about. A trap was set but no bear was caught.

September 9, 2001 (Black Bear, GMU 29, Boulder Co.) A 28-year-old hearing-impaired man was walking his service dog off-leash on the Skunk Creek Trail. He stopped for a break and saw a small, black furry animal feeding in the brush several yards in front of him. He realized it was a bear cub at about the same time that something hit him from behind, knocking him into some bushes. A sow black bear held the man down for a few seconds, tearing his clothes as she pulled away. The sow and cubs then ran back into the brush. The hiker sustained minor scratches and a strained knee. Wildlife officers and Boulder Open Space rangers searched the area but did not find the sow or cubs. Because the incident was deemed "non-aggressive", the black bear was not tracked and destroyed.

October 5, 2001 (Black Bear, GMU 791, Alamosa Co.) A 20-year-old man was camping with several other people just outside the boundary of the Great Sand Dunes National Monument. While most in his camping party slept in tents, the man and a friend slept outside. At approximately 4 A.M., a small- to medium-sized black bear bit the man on the right foot. At first the man thought it was his friends pulling a prank but when he started to speak the bear ran off into the nearby woods. The bear was tracked but not found.

June 29, 2002 (Black Bear, GMU 591, El Paso Co.) An 11-year-old boy was sleeping in a tent by himself on a Boy Scout camping trip at Camp Falcon. He was awakened early in the morning when his tent began to collapse as something stood on top of him. The bear ripped the tent open, stuck its head inside the tent and bit the boy on the right leg. The boy yelled "Bear!" and some of the adults asked if he was ok[ay]. The boy said "yes" and the adults instructed the boy to go back to sleep. Later that morning they discovered that the boy had been bitten and sustained a puncture wound to the thigh. A medium-sized black bear was caught in a culvert trap on July 1 and euthanized.

August 19-20, 2002 (Black Bear, GMU 46, Park Co.) Several groups of students from Jefferson County Open School had an encounter with a black bear while they were camped in the Mount Evans Wilderness Area. On the 19th, the first group of students set up two tents and several tarps that some of the students would be sleeping under. Approximately 1 A.M., one of students sleeping under a tarp saw a bear approaching. The bear took the boy's shoe and started to lick and chew on the shoe. The bear then tore down the tarp the boy was under before a few students were able to scare the bear away from the camp. All the students sat in one of the tents waiting for the bear to leave. The bear proceeded to tear up the camp for about an hour before it came to the tent they were in, striking it. A student was hit in the head but it was unknown if he was struck by the bear or another student in the chaos. The camp was reported to have been very clean before the bear encounter and a Forest Service employee cleaned up the camp after the encounter.

On the 20th, a second group of students were camped under tarps within $1/4$ mile area. About 10:30 P.M., one of the students saw a bear smelling around the area. The bear approached the student and lied down near him. The student got out of his sleeping bag and started to yell. A group leader gathered all the students and kept them near camp as the bear tore up the camp. The bear left the second group of students and went to an area where a third group was camping in tents. The bear came up to the group leader's tent and tried to get into it. When unsuccessful,the bear jumped on the tent, breaking the tent poles. The bear moved between tents and tarps, scratching and chasing one student in the process. As students in the third group were gathered up, the bear began to circle the group. The bear made a bluff charge towards the group. The group did spray the bear with pepper spray but it only affected the bear for a short amount of time. The bear continued to tear up the camps and left around 4:30 A.M. Wildlife officers investigated these incidents but were unable to locate the bear.

August 22, 2002. (Black Bear, GMU 59, Teller Co.) A subadult bear came down on top of a tent and inadvertently put a one-inch scratch on the head of the male sleeping in the tent. Toiletries were in the tent at the time of the incident. The bear had reportedly entered into at least three tents in a two-week period. The bear was shot and killed by a campground resident.

July 13, 2003 (Black Bear, GMU 20, Larimer Co.) Two people were injured by a black bear near Fern Lake in the Rocky Mountain National Park backcountry. A park ranger warned the campers about black bears in the area. The campers took precautions by hanging cooking utensils and trash between two trees away from their campsite. They also kept no food in their tents. Despite the efforts of the four men in the camping party, an aggressive bear slashed through a tent and bit one of the men on the forehead. The man's screams scared away the 250-pound, cinnamon-colored bear, but the bruin headed for one of his companion's tents as the second man continued to sleep. The second man received lacerations that required 30 staples in his skull. The bear ambled into the forest after its victims started screaming. About an hour after the initial incident, witnesses spotted the same bear striking a food-storage container at another campsite in the area. Park officials closed that portion of the park and a trap was set but the bear was never captured.

July 22, 2003. (Black Bear, GMU 28, Grand Co.) A man sleeping in a sleeping bag near his truck was stirred by some noise and woke to a bear looking over him. The man was startled and lifted his head. The bear scratched the man. He jumped into his truck and honked the horn, causing the bear to flee the area. The camper did not require medical attention. The bear was not located.

July 5, 2004 (Black Bear, GMU 521, Gunnison Co.) A federal wildlife agent was attacked by a problem black bear he was tracking. The agent was using dogs to track the bear, which had been killing sheep in the area. The dogs treed the bear. The agent shot and wounded the bear. It fell from the tree and grabbed the man by the leg, biting him while pulling him off of his feet. The man shot the bear in the chest. The bear continued to fight with the dogs and the man, inflicting several additional bite wounds to the man's legs before the bullet wounds resulted in the bear's death. The agent suffered a leg injury but was able to walk back to his camp. A U.S. Forest Service ranger came to his aid and he was taken to Delta County Hospital and treated for bites on all four limbs.

July 28, 2004 (Black Bear, GMU 43, Pitkin Co.) An adult black bear pawed the outside of the tent of a 19-year-old woman. As the bear pawed at the tent, the tent collapsed on the woman and the bear proceeded to roll her around and sniff her. After finding no food in the tent the bear left the area. The woman sustained no serious injuries, but was treated at the hospital for a small wound on the top of her leg and some bruises. Wildlife officers searched the area for several days but could not locate the bear.

August 8, 2004 (Black Bear, GMU 191, Larimer Co.) A woman encountered a bear on her porch. When she opened the door to the porch the bear swiped at her right foot leaving scratch marks. The woman later reported the bear had stepped on her foot. The woman sustained only minor injuries that did not require medical attention. The incident was treated as a non-aggressive encounter, therefore the bear was not tracked and destroyed.

August 10, 2004 (Black Bear, GMU 31, Garfield Co.) An adult, female,black bear was in a cabin when it was startled by the cabin owner's friend. The bear subsequently bit the left foot of the individual and then retreated. The bear had been in the cabin numerous times eating bird grain, flour and cocoa. The sow was later trapped and euthanized.

August 31, 2004 (Black Bear, GMU 62, Montrose Co.) A sheepherder shot and wounded a 200-pound black bear after finding the sow and her cub in the sheep. The sow attacked the herder's dog after being wounded. The herder did not have any more bullets so he picked up a branch and began beating her with it. The sow bit the herder on his leg and arm during the melee. Both the sow and cub were killed by the herder.

September 11, 2004 (Black Bear, GMU 54, Gunnison Co.) An elk hunter was sitting on a stump waiting for daylight when a black bear came up from behind and swatted him on his left shoulder. The hunter was knocked to the ground and the bear immediately ran away from the area. The hunter sustained only minor injuries that did not require medical attention.

July 19, 2005 (Black Bear, GMU 691, Fremont Co.) A 14-year-old Texas boy was treated and released for injuries suffered in an attack by a medium-sized black bear. At approximately 1 A.M., the boy and his 12-year-old cousin were sleeping in a tent at a private campground near Coaldale when the bear scratched through the side of the tent. The boy was bitten on the left hand and received some other scratches and bruises during a brief struggle. Family members sleeping in a nearby hard-sided camper took the boy to a Salida hospital where he received treatment for his injuries. A medium-sized, adult, male black bear was captured and destroyed by wildlife officers.

July 31, 2005 (Black Bear, GMU 581, Teller Co.) A 49-year-old man suffered multiple lacerations on his head and back when he was mauled by a black bear. The man was sleeping in a semi-permanent motor home parked on vacant land north of Cripple Creek when the bear entered through a makeshift pet door around 3 A.M. The man was treated and released from a medical facility in Woodland Park. A trap was set but the bear was not captured.

September 19, 2005 (Black Bear, GMU 59, El Paso Co.) A large black bear injured an 85-year-old woman in the Skyway subdivision in Colorado Springs. The bear frequently visited the woman[']s yard to eat from a large bucket of sunflower seeds that had been placed on a picnic table to feed birds, squirrels, and other wildlife. According to the woman, at least four bears, including the one that bit her, were frequent visitors. A trap was set, but the bear was not captured.

April 26, 2006 (Black Bear, GMU 851, Las Animas Co.) Upon exiting an outhouse, a 29-year-old ranch hand was swatted to the ground by a cinnamon-colored black bear. The man was knocked to the ground but got up quickly and entered his nearby car. Once inside the car the man started the engine and rolled up the windows that had been left down. The bear sniffed around the windows and chewed on the tires until the man drove away. The man was treated and released from a Pueblo hospital for bruises and possible nerve damage to his neck and shoulder. Prior to striking the man, the bear had eaten the man's lunch that was left in his car. A trap was set, but the bear was not captured.

June 17, 2006 (Black Bear, GMU 59, El Paso Co.) A large black bear injured a 17-year-old boy who was camping with his family in a dispersed campsite in the National Forest just outside the Crags Campground. The boy was in a sleeping bag when he felt the bear tugging at the foot of the bag. Initially he thought it was his brother playing a trick on him, but he woke up and realized it was a bear. The boy yelled and the bear landed a glancing blow to the boy's head. The boy was treated and released from a local medical facility for a laceration to his skull requiring several stitches. A short time later, the bear was caught in one of the traps wildlife officers set inside the campground. The boy, and other members of his family, identified the bear as the same one that was at their campsite.

Earlier in the week, a female jogger had been chased by a bear in the Crags Campground area. While investigating the incident with the jogger, the Crags Campground host informed wildlife officers that a 31-year-old man had been bitten on the foot on June 4. The man was reportedly sleeping in his sleeping bag on a chair outside. The man suffered minor injuries and was treated and released from a local hospital. Because of the bear activity in the area, multiple traps were set in the campground and the campground was closed. Wildlife officers and volunteers posted warning signs and talked to hikers and other recreational users in the area. A 190-pound adult male bear was captured and destroyed several days later.

July 15, 2006 (Black Bear, GMU 41, Mesa Co.) At approximately 6:30 A.M. a woman sleeping in her tent felt something grab the covers from her feet. When she sat up, she saw a bear and screamed. The bear swiped at the woman's leg causing gashes that required several stitches. The woman lay still until the bear left the area. The area was closed to camping for several days while wildlife personnel attempted to catch the bear.

March 30, 2007 (Black Bear, GMU 391, Jefferson Co.) A 38-year-old woman suffered abrasions and cuts on the side of her body and legs when a yearling black bear attacked her on her porch. At approximately 12:30 A.M. the woman was in the process of bringing her dogs into the house when the attack occurred. Jefferson County Sheriff's deputies assisted a wildlife officer in the search for the bear. A small (yearling) bear was tracked a short distance away from the scene and observed to be blonde in color. Two other bears, at least one being a yearling and black in color, were also observed close to the scene. The lone blonde bear began to walk down the hill toward the other bears but turned to charge the wildlife officer, who shot and killed the charging bear. After the first shot, the black in color yearling charged the officer. The officer shot toward the bear, which turned and ran. The woman was treated and released from a metro Denver hospital.

September 21, 2007 (Black Bear, GMU 75, La Plata Co.) A landowner suffered a broken nose and some abrasions when a sow swatted him in his face. The adult, male landowner confronted the sow and her cub that had broken in chicken feed in a storage shed. When confronted, the sow grabbed the man's dog by the hind leg. The man was able to grab his dog and start pulling it from the bear. The bear hit the man on the arm and swatted him on the face, breaking his nose. A wildlife officer shot and killed both the sow and cub. The man was treated and released from a local hospital.

October 11, 2007 (Black Bear, GMU 43, Pitkin Co.) A homeowner suffered a number of abrasions on his back and left calf when an adult, boar black bear swatted him in his garage. The homeowner kept dog food inside the garage next to the garage entry door to the home. Early in the morning, the man went to feed his dogs. He flipped on a garage light, startling a bear that was eating dog food next to the door. The homeowner turned immediately to go back in the house when the bear swatted him on the back and the calf. The bear remained in the garage for a short time. The man was treated and released from a local hospital. The garage door had been left up approximately two feet to allow the dogs to go in and out. A wildlife officer shot and killed the bear after it exited the garage. The bear's teeth were well worn and indicated that the bear was older.

October 13, 2007 (Black Bear, GMU 85, Las Animas Co.) An elk hunter was knocked to the ground from behind by a bear. The hunter was able to roll to his back, kicking at the bear and firing his rifle. The bear turned away and the man shot the bear, knocking it to the ground. The bear immediately regained its feet and continued to run as the hunter fired two more shots toward the bear. The man backed down a hill into a small draw while reloading his rifle but could no longer see or hear the bear. The back of the man's shirt was ripped and he sustained minor welts and abrasions. The bear, although wounded, was never located after extensive search and the use of Wildlife Services tracking dogs.

October 16, 2007 (Black Bear, GMU 43, Pitkin Co.) A bear entered a ground-level condo on the west side of Aspen through a slider door that was left unlocked. The bear was in a small kitchen area eating out of the refrigerator. A woman in the condo entered the kitchen to investigate some noises. She came around the corner of the hallway to the kitchen. At that point, the woman was standing between the refrigerator in the small kitchen area and the door the bear had entered. The bear stood up on its hind legs and swatted the homeowner across the head and face. The bear then exited the door it had entered. A trap was set at the condo shortly after the incident. The bear was euthanized by wildlife officers on Oct. 27.

August 10, 2009 (Black Bear, GMU 471, Pitkin Co.) At approximately 10:10 P.M. a woman had gone to the main floor of her Aspen home to work in her home office. As she passed through the house's entryway, her small dog began barking frantically. The woman confronted a large bear. The woman screamed and turned to open the front door to get the dark brown bear out of the house. The bear struck the woman leaving lacerations on her back and chest. The homeowner was able to flee to the upstairs bedroom and call 911. The bear remained in the home for a short time but left as police responded. Wildlife officers arrived a short time later and began efforts to locate the bear. It was determined that the bear gained entry to the home by physically forcing open a pair of French doors. Wildlife officers found no bear attractants around the property that might have guided the offending bear to the location. Based on the description of the bear and the method of entry, officers believed that the same bear was responsible for several other home entries in the area. Several days later, a large, dark brown, male black bear returned the scene and was euthanized.

August 31, 2009 (Black Bear, GMU 47, Pitkin Co.) Around 3 p.m. a woman sleeping on her deck was awakened by a sharp pain in her leg. She immediately awoke to find a bear had inflicted a puncture wound on her leg by either biting or scratching her. The woman reported that she jumped up, prompting the bear to leave the deck area. The bear remained in the yard until wildlife officers and Aspen police responded to the scene. As law enforcement units arrived, the bear went into a tree on the property. The 2-year-old female bear was euthanized.

September 10, 2009: (Black Bear, GMU 43, Pitkin Co.) Shortly after 8 P.M. a homeowner heard his dogs barking. A large, black-colored bear had entered through an unlocked and ajar entry door. The dogs had the bear trapped against the door at the base of some stairs. The bear backed against the door and pushed it closed. The homeowner went down the stairs and grabbed his dogs, trying to protect them. He brought the dogs up the stairs. The bear had no escape route but up the stairs. The homeowner tried to push a chair in front of the bear to stop it. The bear swatted him across the side of the head. The man opened a kitchen window and the bear left out that window. The man was treated and released from a local hospital. Wildlife officers set a trap for the bear at the site and patrolled the neighborhood, but the bear involved in the incident was never located.

June 18, 2010 (Black Bear, GMU 45, Eagle Co.) A 25-year-old Florida man working construction for the summer was taking a walk on his 9 A.M. break when he spooked a large bear. The startled bear charged the man. After the bear hit him once near his left eye and temple, the man put up his arm to protect himself. The bear scratched his left arm, and then knocked the man to the ground, unconscious. When he regained consciousness the bear was gone and the man, covered in bear hair, ran back to his jobsite to get help from his coworkers. The man suffered a black eye and minor cuts and bruises. He was treated and released from a local hospital. The man described the bear as black with a reddish head and estimated the bear to be 350 pounds. Wildlife officers arrived and began efforts to locate the bear using tracking dogs. The dogs picked up the bear's scent at the scene and the bear was located within 300 yards of the incident. The bear left the immediate area and was tracked by officers for about 12 hours. While tracking the bear officers could see the bear a few times, but because of nearby homes they could not safely capture or euthanize the bear. Officers found large amounts of food trash in a roll off construction dumpster at the site of the original incident.

July 8, 2010 (Black Bear, GMU 461, Park Co.) A 51-year-old Bailey man who discovered a bear in his home suffered bite wounds when he approached the animal in his basement. The family heard sounds in their kitchen soon after midnight and realized that a bear had entered the home. The man was bitten on the lower left leg and scratched on the right leg as the bear tried to get past him. A 320-pound, male black bear was shot and killed by wildlife officers outside the house. The man was treated and released from a local hospital. The garage door had been left open and a trash can and a refrigerator inside the garage likely attracted the bear. The door from the home to the garage appeared to have a broken latch.

July 9, 2010 (Black Bear, GMU 84, Custer Co.) At approximately 2 P.M. a man and his dog were walking down a trail when the man saw a dark brown, 300-400 pound black bear feeding in the trail. The dog growled at the bear and the bear ran off. The dog pursued the bear over a hill. The bear then appeared running down the hill toward the man, closing on him at a very rapid rate. The man jumped behind a small Aspen tree to place the tree between him and the bear. The man reported that the bear stood up and acted like it was sniffing or looking to see what was behind the tree. The bear then struck the man on top of the head, knocking him to the ground. The man's dog chased the bear back up the hill. The man fired a shot from his handgun toward the bear. The man sustained a minor injury on the top of his head that did not require medical attention. Wildlife officers tried to locate the bear involved but were unsuccessful.

July 10, 2010: (Black Bear, GMU 74, La Plata Co.) At approximately 2:30 A.M., two men sleeping outside a local soup kitchen were awakened by a bear grabbing their blanket. The bear bit one of the men on the arm, the pair were able to escape into a nearby building. The bear's bite did not break the skin, though there were visible indentations where the bear's canine teeth sank into the man's arm. Wildlife officers say there are several transient camps near where the attack occurred, and bears can be attracted because they have easy access to trash and food. Officers with tracking dogs found the bear 300 yards from the incident, and shot and killed it. The two men and another witness identified the bear from the attack. A necropsy on the 200-250 pound, male black bear revealed trash and human food in its digestive system.

July 15, 2010 (Black Bear, GMU 73, Montezuma Co.) At approximately 1 A.M., a 14-year-old boy and his 12-year-old sister were sleeping in their backyard in a residential neighborhood south of Cortez. They were awakened by a sub-adult black bear. The bear bit the boy, who screamed and shined a flashlight at the bear. The bear ran from the area. Paramedics treated the boy at the scene for a bite wound that punctured the skin. The girl didn't realize that the bear had bit her until later, when her arm became bruised. The bruise did not require treatment. Wildlife officers were notified and were on the scene by 2 A.M. Tracking dogs were utilized to locate the bear but were unsuccessful.

July 24, 2010 (Black Bear, GMU 28, Grand Co.) At approximately 6 A.M., a 16-year-old boy was awakened by a bear licking the boy's face. The bear then bit the boy's face. The boy sustained minor gashes and several small puncture wounds on his head. He did not require medical attention. A trap was set near the location. An adult female bear matching the description was captured and destroyed within 24 hours of the incident.

May 31, 2011 (Black Bear, GMU 66, Hinsdale Co.) A 41-year-old man riding a bike northbound near a store parking lot around 7:30 P.M. was clawed by a sow bear. The man saw two yearling cubs going southbound through the same parking lot but never saw the sow. The sow left the area with the cubs immediately after the contact with the bicyclist. The man did not require medical attention. The incident was treated as a non-aggressive encounter; therefore the bear was not tracked and destroyed.

June 29, 2011 (Black Bear, GMU 74, La Plata Co.) At approximately 4:30 A.M., a man sleeping outside near a local soup kitchen was awakened by a bear close to his sleeping bag. The man lay still as the bear sniffed a bag of clothes before it began sniffing at the sleeping bag. The bear nudged the man's feet and began chewing at the bag. The man then jumped up and yelled at the bear. The bear bit the man's left wrist and palm and lunged back. Using his camp mattress as a shield between him and the bear, the man backed up slowly before turning to run down a hill away from the bear. The man was treated and released at a local hospital for minor puncture wounds and abrasions. Wildlife officers found trash next to the attack site and at several nearby transient camps. Wildlife Services personnel with tracking dogs found and treed a black bear matching the description of the offending bear, 100 yards from where the incident occurred. The bear was killed by Wildlife officers at approximately 11:45 A.M. the same day as the attack. The 290-pound boar was missing its right canines, which is consistent with the man's injuries.

July 5, 2011 (Black Bear, GMU 84, Huerfano Co.) A bear entered a home through an open kitchen window at approximately 2:50 A.M. The homeowner tried using an air horn to haze the bear through a door she had opened when the bear ran over her. The bear exited the house through the open door and was chased away by the homeowner's dogs. The woman sustained two deep facial lacerations on the bridge of her nose and to the right of her right eye, and four superficial scratches near her shoulder blades. She was treated and released from a local hospital. A site inspection found several other open windows and an open sliding glass door along with a large sack of dog food near the door of the dining room adjacent to the kitchen. Wildlife officers set two bear traps at the site and in the neighborhood, but the bear was not captured.

July 15, 2011 (Black Bear, GMU 48, Lake Co.) At approximately 3:30 A.M. a 13-year-old boy sleeping in a tent with his 15-year-old cousin was awakened when a bear bit his leg. The boy's screams woke up other campers, who helped chase the bear out of the immediate area. The boy was treated and released at an area hospital for minor scratches on his right elbow and deep lacerations on his left leg sustained in the attack. Before it came into the boy's tent, the bear had been rummaging through coolers around the campsite, which was part of a larger gathering of campers. Wildlife Services personnel with tracking dogs found a 200-pound male black bear matching the description of the offending bear within three quarters of a mile from the incident and euthanized it shortly before 7 P.M. the same day.

August 19, 2011 (Black Bear, GMU 43, Pitkin Co.) At approximately 5:30 A.M., two men sleeping in a tent were awoken by a bear circling their tent. The bear stood up on its hind legs before landing on top of the occupied tent, collapsing the tent and pinning the occupants. One of the men lay still under the bear in the collapsed tent and was bitten in the back of his leg by a bear when he moved. The man sustained a couple of minor puncture wounds on his left leg that did not require immediate medical attention. The campers were able to scare the bear off by shouting at it. The campers indicated that their food was stored high in a tree at least 75 feet from their campsite. The men reported the attack to the US Forest Service the next day.

August 20, 2011 (Black Bear, GMU 43, Pitkin Co.) At approximately 1 A.M., a 51-year-old man was awakened by a bear biting his sleeping bag and leg. The man was able to fight the bear off and called for help to his fellow campers sleeping in nearby tents. Despite repeated attempts to scare the bear away, it would not leave immediate area. The three men watched the bear circling the campsite the remainder of the night. The man sustained substantial non life-threatening injuries to his lower right leg, and was able to walk with assistance to meet Mountain Rescue Aspen members on a nearby trail. Rescue members transported the man to a local hospital where he was treated for his injuries. The man reported having an empty bag of freeze-dried food inside a backpack in his tent. Wildlife Services personnel with tracking dogs successfully tracked and found a 200-pound male black bear matching the description of the offending bear $1^{1}/_{2}$ miles from the incident and euthanized it at approximately 7 A.M. August 21. The same bear is believed to have also been involved in the August 19 attack less than two miles away.

August 21, 2011 (Black Bear, GMU 81, Conejos Co.) A man who discovered a bear eating sunflower seeds from a trashcan on his deck suffered lacerations when he tried to haze the animal. The incident occurred at approximately 10:30 P.M. when the man went onto his deck 10 feet away from the bear and used a piece of firewood to bang on a trashcan lid to try and scare the bear away. It was at that time the bear lunged towards the man knocking him into the wall of his cabin as he turned away from the bear. The man then went back into his cabin and locked the door. The man sustained a laceration to his right ear and a 2-inch long scratch on the left side of his neck, and was treated and released from a local hospital. Wildlife Services personnel with tracking dogs successfully tracked and found a male black bear matching the description of the offending bear $1^{1}/_{2}$ miles from the incident and euthanized it at approximately 10:30 P.M. August 22. The property had both liquid and seed bird feeders around the cabin.

September 6, 2011 (Black Bear, GMU 36, Eagle Co.) A man walking his dog in the evening was attacked by a bear.

When the bear slapped the man, he was thrown to the ground dislocating his right shoulder. The man also sustained bruises to the left side of his face and two scratches near his mouth. The man was reluctant to report the incident and did not seek medical attention. The man reported that four different bears, a sow with two cubs and a boar, had been around the trailer park all summer, getting into trash. An inspection of the man's trailer lot found no trash. Wildlife officers set a bear [sic] in the trailer park but after several days no bear was captured and the trap was pulled.

Sanctuary

THE TWO BEAR cubs are fighting—tumbling and galloping over each other like brothers—although in fact, they've come from different parts of the state, and they should be hibernating right now. Instead they are wrestling in the snow at the Pauline S. Schneegas Wildlife Foundation in Silt, Colorado, and it occurs to me that their playfulness is a far shout from what they would have been, which is dead.

I'm touring the only privately licensed facility in Colorado that shelters and rehabilitates bears (along with cougars, bobcats, and other Colorado wildlife). Snow-capped peaks surround the outbuildings and fenced areas, and the view is spectacular. Mainly, though, I'm entranced by the animals: "Robby," "Bobby," "Mollie," and "Lollipop," the four bobcats which were someone's illegal pets until they were confiscated; "Furry Murie," the artic fox; "Annie," a mountain lion who used to belong to a man who'd illegally purchased her; a redtailed hawk, a kestrel, a coyote.

And how did the bears get here? One had a broken leg after being hit by a car (his mother and sibling died), the other had been abandoned by its mother because it was weak—it had severe pneumonia and a heart murmur. Right now, they're hanging off a tire swing and pawing at some apples in the snow underneath it. As I stamp my feet to warm up, I notice that they looked about as happy, warm, and oblivious as two young creatures can be. They've got a few more months of sanctuary left, and then, it's time for release into the larger sanctuary of wildness.

MANY CONSIDER the Schneegas Foundation to be "bear experts," in that they've experimented so much with the best way of releasing bears. The scenario usually goes like this: bear cubs are brought in by Colorado Parks and Wildlife or by others. Often, the mothers have been hit by a car, euthanized for being an offender bear, or have died from other causes. Once at the facility, the cubs are fed until they're about 120 pounds, and then, in late February or early March, CPW personnel and volunteers will snowmobile to a remote area and build a snow cave, or release each bear into an area with lots of heavy timber. The bears will naturally go into hibernation and come out in April or May, when the aspens are "flowering" and the cubs have a good chance of surviving in the wild.

"If we can time it so that they'll be released right before a blizzard, and let the snow come, the bears will stay put. We try to work with what their natural cycles would have been," explained Nanci Limbach, who started this foundation and named it in honor of her grandmother. "We were the first ones in the United States to do these winter releases, and they're highly successful."

These two cubs will be released in the spring—after they've gained enough weight in order to ensure a successful transition. "Instinct will kick in for them," Nanci said. "It always does."

THE BEARS are lucky in that regard—some of the animals here are *not* releasable. The bobcats, for instance, are required by law to stay. "We can't just take animals out to the wild and dump them. We need to know where they came from, and we need to know they'll survive, we need to know it's appropriate," Al King said. He's brother to Nanci, and chairman of the foundation board. "These bobcats have been raised as pets; they've been declawed; and they have degenerative disease from poor nutrition. They can't be released. We're against having animals in captivity, but the ones that need to be kept here we use as teaching animals for conservation education. If we can teach just one person, then these animals have served a purpose." These bobcats, then, are ambassadors for all wrongfully adopted "pet" wildlife—people generally buying or capturing small animals when they're cute and furry, only to realize they grow up to be...well, wild.

Whether an animal is in need of rehabilitation, a home, or release, all species of wildlife are accepted at the Schneegas Foundation if brought in from Colorado. In total, they've taken care of dozens of bears. In 2010, for example, they released nineteen into the wild. They've had as many as twenty-five bear residents at one time.

To make this all happen, the foundation relies on the good will of others. Dr. Paul Bingham, a vet from Fruita, helps with the vet work and medicines. Other volunteers come in to feed, care, and help rehabilitate. The food is the major cost—upwards of $60,000 a year. Food donations also help—CPW might bring in a road-killed elk, which is enough for only one day's feed, but still helpful; local orchards donate apples, which volunteers pick and transport.

While the Schneegas Foundation works closely with CPW, they don't get any funding from them, or from any other local government or animal control departments. The two groups, however, have a long-standing relationship. The foundation has someone bringing them bears that need help, and CPW has a place to take animals that need homes. Kevin Wright, the CPW manager in nearby Aspen, has taken several bears there, especially in the summer of 2009—a notoriously bad drought year—when there "were so many conflicts and we had to euthanize so many bears."

Some of these situations, he added, can be complicated. For example, there was one bear taken to the foundation—a yearling that was "skin and bones, severely malnourished." A resident had found it and tried to feed it without success, and the bear was picked up by Pitkin County Animal Control. The bear was taken to Nanci's and was nursed back to health, then and released the next winter.

In cases such as this, is human interference the right thing? As Wright noted, that sort of situation raises several questions. "Is that what should happen? It was well meant by all involved.... When there is a natural food failure, there will be increased natural mortality, especially among cubs and yearlings. That is nature's population control. Is it right to interfere with that? Nature can be cruel at times." He went on to say that the use of a "rehabber" should come when the bear is orphaned by human-related causes—not nature. "That may sound cruel and cold-hearted," he added, "but sometimes I wonder if a cub without the sow, who is then placed with humans—well, hopefully, it doesn't habituate to humans. Would it have been better served to humanely euthanize that cub?"

Wright sees a need for rehabilitation, though: "Rehabilitation has its place, it is needed, and it is the last chance these animals have to survive. I despise having to put bears (or other wildlife) down. Sometimes we have to, sometimes it's to stop suffering, and sometimes an animal needs to be put down because of its aggressiveness toward people. Doesn't mean I have to like it." He added that it's simply good to be realistic about the situation. "When we release younger bears, we are releasing them in another's territory and there are larger bears," he said. "Males will kill younger bears. On the other hand, it's these bears' only chance to survive. Without the facility and Nanci and Al, many of these bears would be euthanized. Nanci works so hard and is truly dedicated to her work. She gives them a chance to be a bear."

Before leaving the facility, I asked around for favorite bear stories. Jon Wilson, who does a lot of building and maintenance there, recalled a little "nineteen-pounder," that he had named "Tubby" (for "obvious reasons," he said. "Man, that bear had a tummy!") Jon shrugged and smiled and looked up into the mountains. "I guess I was a little worried he wouldn't make it. He'd been so little. But spotters found him as an adult. He had a female. What's better for a bear than a home range, a partner, and a future?"

Nanci has had some favorite bears too. "We have a couple of tri-pod bears out there, with three legs. One time, two cubs came in—it was suspected that their mom was killed by a male bear, and the male went after the cubs, too. One had gangrene in a leg, another had a missing eye. So we had One Eye and Tri Pod." She also recalled "Boo-boo Bear," who was brought in severely underweight. She'd been told he was under six months, but he was clearly over a year, so she named him "Boo-boo" because of the mistake. "That bear was just fun to watch. It would lay in the sunshine. It *loved* sunshine. He got released, and we never heard from him again. Not hearing anything is a good story. No news is good news."

There was one tragedy: A few years ago, Nanci and Jon had driven a bear way out to a safe location. "We said to him, 'Head west, head west, young man!' Nanci said. "The *very* next day lightning started a wildfire. The fire caused the animals to head into town, and this bear headed right into Gateway, and a man shot it. What are the chances of a fire that night? That is a tragedy. That was a freak of nature."

But all in all, "It's a pretty good system," Al said to me, as we stood in the middle of the snow-packed yard, amid all the animals. "They go on to lead pretty happy bear lives."

"They look pretty happy now, too," I commented. "Like they don't want to cause trouble."

"Oh boy," Al said. "No kidding. I'd rather handle a bear than a raccoon any day."

Then he paused and added, "Watching them go is what it's all about. People ask if I get sad when they leave. I'm not sad. The only reason these animals are here in the first place is because humans interfered. It's best that they're back out where they belong." Al stood in the yard, surrounded by various animals and the wildness of the Colorado mountains. "I'd like to teach people to put us out of business," he added. "Wouldn't that be great?"

KWIYAGA

THE SOUTHERN UTE BEAR DANCE

IN THE FAR southwestern reaches of Colorado, nearly on the New Mexico border, the Southern Ute Indian Reservation spreads across 1,058 square miles in La Plata, Archuleta, and Montezuma counties. The reservation is well off the beaten path—possibly the most remote and difficult inhabited place in all of Colorado to get to—and my journey there involved several mountain passes, several spring snowstorms, and several stops to get out and stretch my back. Once in the town of Ignacio, I drove past the beautiful new Ute Cultural Center and the new casino—I wanted to visit both—but first I needed to see the Bear Dance. Following uncertain directions, I headed out of town to the river, got lost a few times, and eventually ended up at the dancing grounds, where the Bear Dance had been going on for a few days. I heard the soul-deep beat of music before I saw the dancers, and it did, somehow, seem a herald of spring and rejuvenation, and an honoring of Mother Earth and of the bears that were leaving their dens and re-entering the world.

This dance is one of the most important annual ceremonies for the tribe, according to Matthew Box, an elder and the Bear Dance Chief of the Southern Ute Tribe. I found him standing in white dress shirt and black pants and vest jacket at the edge of the dance, preparing to announce a new set of dancers. He noted that the Bear Dance has a social side to it (as opposed to the Sun Dance) and its importance is several-fold, ultimately providing a means in which to "shed luggage." The dance, Box noted, "welcomes the spring and the life it brings," adding that bears are "sacred to our tribe and are not killed or hunted, not eaten, nor are their hides or any part of the bear used in any way." And if ever there is an encounter with a bear, then "talking to the bear as a brother or sister is the answer, although common sense goes a *very* long way."

According to some, the Bear Dance is the oldest known continuous dancing tradition in North America, dating back much longer than the 15th century, when Spanish explorers first witnessed the ceremony and recorded it. According to many, the origin story goes like this: There were two brothers out hunting, and one of the brothers noticed a bear standing upright, facing a tree, dancing and making a noise while clawing the tree. He stayed to watch the bear, while the other brother went to hunt. As a favor to the one watching, the bear taught him to perform this dance, and told the man that he should teach it to his people so that they could show respect for the bear and draw from the bear's strong spirit.

Versions vary, but in one rendition, members of the tribe danced each spring to rouse their bear relatives from hibernation, and spirit messengers traveled from bear den to bear den, gently coaxing the snoozing inhabitants from their slumber. With the loud chanting, dancing, and music, the groggy bears were fully awakened. And in return for this wakeup call, the Native Americans receive friendship and protection from the bears, and the bears use their supernatural powers to help the tribe. It was also believed that in addition to great wisdom, bears possess immortal invulnerability—which makes sense, given their repeated return to the world after disappearing all winter. It was also believed that bears had healing powers and that they knew the secrets of medicinal herbs, and again, it's easy to see where such beliefs originated, since bears eat such a broad array of plants, berries, and roots.

According to some stories, it was also believed that Native Americans would change back into bears upon death. As such, the dance had another purpose, which was to send messages to deceased loved ones. The bears were believed to be able to communicate directly with the spirit world.

Today, the dance is held annually on Memorial Day weekend in May. "Before my time, it was held in March to coincide with the time in which the bear came out of hibernation," Box told me, but the dance was moved to a later date, when the weather is better and the local schools are out for the summer. It is indeed quite crowded—200 people, I'm guessing, either dancing, milling about watching, chatting, and generally welcoming the spring.

I watched as new dancers filtered into the corral, where they formed two lines, one male, one female, facing one another. The women were all wearing dresses and shawls, and many were wearing beaded moccasin boots, although Tevas and tennis shoes were plentiful too. Some of the men were in T-shirts and jeans, some wearing bowler hats, some in ribbon shirts. Then the music started: a group of men opposite began singing and creating a heartbeat-like rhythm with a morache or "growl stick," an instrument made from hard notched wood, and bone or metal. The sound that's created imitates both the noise made by the bear and the first thunder of spring, which is believed to awaken the bears. The Bear Dance songs are now mostly wordless, I discover, although historically singers incorporated bits of previous year's news and gossip, to encourage the dancers and to tease them.

Another important component is the plumes—feathers worn that represent worries and tensions that have built up over the winter. One of the purposes of the dance, then, is to help ease tensions and burdens. On the fourth and final day of the dance, the plumes are left on a cedar tree at the east entrance of the corral. As Box noted, when "the dance is over, anyone who wishes to can leave pain, suffering, bad luck, or 'mental luggage' on a tree inside the corral by putting a plume, fringe, hair tie or anything in general that has been with that person. When walking away, the person does not turn back to look, but literally leaves it there for creation to 'take care of.'"

The dance has important social implications as well. Box noted that the younger people are able to meet possible future life partners, and that "married couples are not allowed to dance with each other" and must "learn how trust, which is key to long-term relationships." He also added that the "older people and tribe in general use this time to gather with other family members who live elsewhere and break bread with them and visit."

Box, who has led the dance for seven years, is following in the footsteps of his grandfather, Eddie Box Sr., who ran the Bear Dance beginning in 1952. "The dance lives on and all are welcome," he noted, adding that other tribes attend, as well as "regulars" from around the world.

He stressed that the dance is not meant to be a tourist event (and indeed, I was the only Anglo-looking woman there at the time), and participants "dance and benefit from the cultural teaching, as we all are the same when it comes to suffering, crying, and dealing with life in general. The dance gives us the tools against our enemies of the world—which are anger, hate, greed, jealousy, violence, drug and ethyl abuse, and the dance provides a means to rejuvenate annually to be at our best. These cultural teachings are needed in all generations and will be necessary for future generations—regardless of McDonald's or the stock market—and which is why it has continued."

With that, he was off to conduct the dance. A huge gust of wind picked up dirt and swept it across the corral, which made children laugh and duck their faces. Before the music started up again, one of the elders spoke into a microphone: "This is a time to look forward to something good, this is a time to move our bodies. Before cars, before even the horse, we danced. There are many distractions nowadays, but this dance helps our people make good tracks on Mother Earth." He smiled at the crowd and then returned to his place as one of the music-makers, and the dancing began. I looked at the dancers swaying their arms, building rhythm, and then beginning to move forward and then backward, the women kicking their feet up as they went backwards, black hair flying, the proud straight backs, and the smiles, and I hoped bears were nearby, listening.

ZEBULON PIKE'S ARREST

A STORY OF SERENDIPITY, FOLLY, AND BEARS

ZEBULON MONTGOMERY PIKE was, in the opinion of many, not exactly the best explorer. He was frequently lost, he and his men often were not prepared, and sometimes he simply suffered from bad luck. In a fairly bizarre sequence of events, he did, however, secure two grizzly cubs, which he recognized as a species different from the black bear, and which he sent to President Thomas Jefferson, thus becoming responsible for the first two grizzlies ever to be publicly exhibited—in the world.

Unlike Lewis and Clark, Zebulon Pike had no specialized training in observation, and lacked formal education—which is why, perhaps, he made no scientific discoveries and had such a twisted journey. He did, however, have an odd penchant for finding disaster, which makes for interesting reading.

On his second expedition out west, Pike was charged with exploring the regions around the Arkansas and Red rivers, which took him into the territory that would later become Colorado. This segment of his journey was perhaps the most difficult in terms of mental resolve and physical stamina, and his group came close to disaster on several occasions. Indeed, reading the account of his journey is reminiscent of looking at a Family Circus cartoon, where dotted lines indicate a child's random path. Yet the time they were in Colorado also proved in many ways to be the group's finest hour—and so it is appropriate, perhaps, that Colorado also contains Pikes Peak, a monument grand enough to recognize the magnitude of their achievements.

The short version of his Colorado journey is this: After a trek across the Great Plains, the expedition entered the future state on November 11, 1806, and made their first camp near the present-day town of Holly. Pike was seeking the source of the Arkansas River, which he found and lost and found again. As an example, at one point, the river split in the mountains, and Pike didn't know what to do. In his journal, he wrote that since the "geography of the country had turned out to be so different from our expectation; we were some what at a loss which course to pursue, unless we attempted to cross the sno cap'd mountains."

Which is what, more less, he did. Food was running out and the men were desperately cold. Crossing over a mountain pass, he came to another river that he thought was the Red. In reality, the expedition was back on the Arkansas, seventy miles upstream from where they had left it two weeks earlier. The men spent Christmas eating buffalo meat near the modern-day town of Salida, with no blankets (their socks having worn out, their blankets had been cut up to improvise socks). And thus the journey went on, this way and that, with one disaster after another—frostbite, hunger, getting lost, and near-mutiny. At one point, in January 1807, nine of the fourteen men suffered from frostbitten feet, including Pike's best hunters. During one blizzard, no one could steady his shaking hands enough to shoot buffalo for food, although Pike finally got one when it ran within point-blank range of his position.

What happened next has been the subject of much lively debate. Did Pike mistakenly or deliberately wander into Spanish territory? Had he made an honest error in mistaking the Rio Grande (generally held to be in Spanish territory) for the Red River (claimed by the U.S. as part of the Louisiana Purchase), or had he deliberately trespassed to spy on the Spanish? In any case, they had left the United States, and Pike and his men were arrested.

After being captured on February 26, 1807, by Spanish authorities in northern New Mexico (now part of Colorado), he and his men were taken to Santa Fe, then to Chihuahua, and then Pike and his men were released to the United States at the Louisiana border on July 1, 1807.

Here is where the bears come in: As the story goes, while Pike was being escorted back through New Spain and to the border of U.S. territory, he purchased the cubs from a local resident. Pike recognized that the grizzly was a different species of bear from that found in the East, and noted in his letter to Jefferson that they were "considered by the natives of that country as the most ferocious animals of the continent," although in a later letter to Jefferson, Pike described how the cubs had followed "my men like dogs through our camps...playing with each other and the soldiers." He asked Jefferson to assure some measure of care for the bears, and finally, as if to calm any fears, he wrote, "they seldom or ever attack a man, unprovoked, but defend themselves courageously."

Thomas Jefferson received the pair of grizzly bears in 1807. Although Pike and Jefferson never met face to face, they did exchange letters during this year.

Jefferson was aware of the grizzly bear, as he had heard first-hand accounts of the western grizzly from Meriwether Lewis and William Clark, who had traveled through the Upper Missouri River's grizzly country in 1805-1806. Jefferson always was intrigued by the western territories, and was fascinated by the knowledge of flora and fauna from the West, but apparently he was not in favor of keeping the bears. In a letter to his granddaughter, Ann Cary Randolph Bankhead, he mentioned the arrival of the cubs from Pike and stated, "These are too dangerous and troublesome for me to keep. I shall therefore send them to Peale's Museum."

Charles Willson Peale, artist and devotee of the natural sciences, was a friend and correspondent of Jefferson's. In 1786 he had opened a museum in Philadelphia that displayed portraits along with a varied collection of natural history objects. In writing to ask Peale to if he would take the two bears, Jefferson stressed that they had been taken as cubs, were "perfectly gentle" and "appear quite good humored."

It took nearly two months to get the cubs to Philadelphia. These two bears became the first grizzlies to be on public display in the world. They didn't last long, however. After arriving at Peale's museum, they were soon after put down, being deemed too dangerous.

And what became of Pike? He was promoted to the rank of brigadier general during the War of 1812, and was killed while commanding his troops during the successful assault on York (now Toronto).

Although his actual journals were confiscated by the Spanish authorities, and not recovered from Mexico until the 1900s, Pike's account of his southwest expedition was published in 1810 as *The Expeditions of Zebulon Montgomery Pike to Headwaters of the Mississippi River, Through Louisiana Territory, and in New Spain, During the Years 1805-6-7*. Pike's journal pales in comparison to the detailed accounts by Lewis and Clark, but the information that Pike brought back about the western plains and the central Rocky Mountains was useful, and it provided interesting reading for a public increasingly curious about the West. And, of course, his travels and arrest serendipitously gave the world her first on-display grizzlies.

The First Death

Here's an interesting fact: The man who has the distinction of being the first European American to be buried in the soil of what became the state of Colorado is also the first white man who was killed by a grizzly there.

In 1821, Lewis Dawson was part of an expedition near the Spanish Peaks, near what is now Trinidad, Colorado. The group was camped on the Purgatory River when they came upon a grizzly. The men were armed with flintlock rifles, but before enough shots had been fired into the bear to kill it, Dawson had been severely mauled.

The journal of expedition leader Jacob Fowler—as printed by Dave Petersen in his wonderful book *Ghost Grizzlies*—gives a unique insight into the event and the times. Indeed, there is nothing more I can add—the story tells itself:

> When it Sprung up and Caught Lewis doson and Pulled Him down in an Instent   Conl glanns gun missed...But a large Slut Which belongs to the Party atacted the Bare With such fury that it left the man and persued Her a few steps in Which time the man got up and Run a few steps but Was overtaken by the bare...the Conl now be Came alarmed lest the Bare Wold pusue Him and Run up Stooping tree—and after Him the Wounded man Was followed by the Bare and thus they Ware all three up one

tree…till the Bare Caught Him by one leg and drew Him back wards down the tree.

Dawson's shredded scalp was "Sewed up as Well as Cold Be don by men In our Situation" and "on examining a Hole in the upper part of His Wright temple Which We believed only Skin deep We found the Brains Workeing out."

Dawson said, "I am killed that I Heard my Skull Brake."

He died three days later.

OLD MOSE

COLORADO'S MOST
FAMOUS BEAR

OLD MOSE, King of the Grizzlies, was arguably the most famous bear ever to have lived in Colorado. Depending on the story, Old Mose killed at least one man or five, thousands of livestock or dozens, and was the biggest grizzly ever killed, or just darn big. The fact that there are so many stories points to one clear truth: he captured the imagination of people everywhere. What we know for sure is that he eluded one obsessed hunter for twenty years, he was missing two back toes, and that when he was shot in 1904, he was one of the largest grizzlies ever recorded. And that in certain wonderful and surprising ways, he was indeed a king of the grizzlies.

THE DEATH of Jacob Radcliff was in fact a tragedy—that much is true. It was 1883 and gold had been discovered. Mining camps were springing up in the mountains of Colorado, and the need for meat was high. Deer and elk meat were in great demand—by the turn of the century, in fact, the state practically had no elk left. And so it came to be that on the morning of November 18, 1883, Jacob Radcliff and a friend left Fairplay and headed into the remote Black Mountain to hunt. The next morning, while the men were on foot, a huge bear came roaring through the underbrush and attacked Radcliff. His ankle and bone legs were shattered, his face was torn open, his back was ripped apart. The friend ran for help, Radcliff was carried to a nearby ranch, and a doctor was summoned. After a great deal of suffering, it all proved to be too late. Just before he died, Radcliff was reported to have said, "Boys, don't hunt that bear."

But hunt the bear they did. One of the men who heard the story was a local resident, the unfortunately-named Mr. Wharton Pigg, who began hunting for this particular grizzly bear in the spring of 1884. He hunted every spring and summer for the next *twenty years*, in fact. He went so far as to buy a ranch—the Stirrup Ranch, which sat right near Black Mountain—and right in the center of Old Mose's route (Old Mose got that name for his moseying, ambling ways). Pigg found other bears, other wildlife, grizzly tracks, bits of hair in branches, and compiled reports from ranchers of various kills. But for summer after summer, trek after trek, Old Mose eluded him.

In 1901, he did succeed at getting two of Old Mose's toes. He'd set a beartrap in a shallow pond where he knew Old Mose loved to splash around—grizzlies are big on playing in water—and here, the trap could be neither seen nor scented. The trap itself weighed nearly fifty pounds, and was hooked to a heavy logging chain ten feet long and tied to a pine log. The jaws of the trap were sixteen inches wide and had three-inch teeth. Several weeks later, a ranch hand did his morning check of the trap and came upon the bear, roaring and thrashing around. The hand rode back to Stirrup Ranch to get others, but by the time they returned, Old Mose was gone. But he had been there, all right—two grizzly bear toes were left behind—but Pigg had succeeded only in giving Old Mose his distinctive footprint.

Wharton Pigg considered Old Mose "his bear," and it was assumed by many that he would be the one to kill it. But in the spring of 1904—twenty long years after Pigg had started his obsessive hunt—a man by the name of James Anthony came to town with thirty hunting dogs. Anthony was a self-proclaimed "professional bear slayer" and one of the many hunters that came from across the country to hunt bears—the last large carnivore around—and this bear in particular. He contacted Pigg—whose own hunting dogs had not been helpful—and they went out together. Old Mose, like all grizzlies, would just have come out of hibernation.

After searching for weeks, they found grizzly tracks (with the distinctive footprint), and circled the area on Black Mountain. Then the dogs caught the scent; Pigg went in the direction he thought the scent led, Anthony stayed with the pack of dogs.

Though Wharton Pigg had been hunting Old Mose for twenty years, it was Anthony who got the shot with his .30-40 carbine. It took several shots, many of which missed the bear entirely—but he finally shot Old Mose at the spot where the spinal cord joined the neck. "He sank down slowly to the ground," Anthony wrote, "raised himself partly up once or twice and was still except for his breathing which continued for some time." Mose never made a sound.

The body of Old Mose was hauled into Cañon City, where supposedly over 2,000 people gathered to see the famous bear. A picture of Wharton Pigg on one side, James Anthony on the other (with his Winchester model 1895 rifle) was taken—many people have commented that the look on Pigg's face is one of dazed sorrow.

The death of Old Mose was huge news. The *Denver Post* of May 15, 1904, printed a full-page article about "The King of the Grizzlies," with a hand-drawn devil-like bear, a drawing of a bear brain, and photos of Mose's home territory. Other highly sensationalized stories followed, with headlines such as "The Grizzly that Terrorized Colorado." Old Mose, even in death, was demonized. The *Cañon City Clipper*, for instance, reported the next day: "Old Mose Dead. The Largest And Oldest Bear Criminal Of Fremont County Finally Killed." The paper continued: "He has killed innumerable calves, cows, colts and other animals, and about twenty years ago he killed Jake Radcliff. Thousands of attempts have been made by hunters with rifle and with trap to get him, but he has born [sic] a charmed life."

Even Enos A. Mills, the early grizzly bear naturalist (the "father of Rocky Mountain National Park"), whose steady and calm observations of bear life regularly defied common thinking of the day, recounts the story with what is probably exaggeration. He wrote, "Old Mose killed at least five men and eight hundred cattle, together with dozens of colts and other live stock. His damage must have exceeded thirty thousand dollars. He had a fiendish habit of slipping up on campers or prospectors, then rushing into their camp with a roar, and he evidently enjoyed the stampedes thus caused." But Mills was also careful to note, "Although he slaughtered stock to excess, he never went out and attacked people. The five men whom he killed were men who had cornered him and were attempting to kill him."

In fact, of the three human deaths (not five) charged to Old Mose, only one, Jake Radcliff, was ever verified (and that anecdotally by his hunting partner); the evidence of the other two were simply skeletons of two missing men found near where the bear was denning.

In any case, for better or worse, the great beast was gone.

Old Mose—who measured eight and a half feet from snout to tail—was skinned and the hide sent to a taxidermist in Colorado Springs to make a rug with the head in an open-mouth mount. The hide still exists, it's said, stashed in the

Wharton Pigg (at left) and James Anthony with the remains of Old Mose.

biological specimen vault at the University of California, Berkeley. Old Mose's skull and brain were sent to a professor at Colorado College in Colorado Springs for study—a few days later, in a letter to the *Denver Post*, he wrote: "One of the most interesting brains I have ever seen lies on the laboratory table before me. It is the brain of Old Mose, the huge grizzly which was recently killed on the hills south of Pikes Peak." He also mentioned the enormous development of the sense of smell, hearing, and motor area.

The carcass was cut up for meat for the residents of Cañon City—and Colorado butcher shops far and wide advertised "Old Mose, ten cents a pound," according to Doug Peacock. The butchers found several old bullets in the body—one was thought to have been fired by Jake Radcliff in 1883, just before the bear killed Radcliff. There were also reports of numerous healed bullet wounds—the commonly reported number is twenty. Some reports say that Old Mose weighed over 3,000 pounds, which would make him the largest grizzly ever recorded, although others say that he was 770 pounds field-dressed, which meant slightly over 1,000 pounds live weight.

He was, as James Perkins writes in his fine book *Old Mose*, "shot at often, hit occasionally, trapped once, and had Wharton Pigg dedicating his life to hunting him down," but in the end, "He was just a grizzly bear that had been given a name and wrapped in a myth."

EVEN SO, the legend of Old Mose lives on. As recently as 2004, *Outdoor Life* magazine proclaimed Old Mose the most famous grizzly ever in their publication. He's also now the mascot of Adams State College in Alamosa, Colorado. A beautiful rendition of the grizzly now sits outside campus—the twelve-foot-high statue was commissioned by Adams State from artist Jim Gilmore, who was born and raised on a cattle ranch near the creature's old stamping grounds. "I had heard of Old Mose before I did the monument," Gilmore told me, "but I researched his history much more before doing the sculpture. I tried to be faithful to the facts and legends about Old Mose, such as him losing two toes on his hind foot in a trap." He's familiar with the land and the legends, too: "I have spent time in the San Juan Mountains where the last grizzly in Colorado was found, and I still hope there is a remote canyon somewhere in that area where a couple of grizzlies can still be found. It would just seem to make Colorado a better place than it already is."

When I traveled to Alamosa to stand beneath the statue, I looked around at the mountains of his home range, and I thought of a hundred years ago, when the giant bears still roamed the Colorado mountains. In Old Mose's honor, I made a wish that indeed, perhaps there will be a day in these parts when grizzlies are more than myth or folktale.

Old Mose

By Emma Ghent Curtis

There is told of Poncha mountain
And they that listen quail—
A story grim as an ogre's whim
And wild as a were-wolf tale.

O, never did tale of were-wolf
On a Gascon peasant's lip
Describe more woes than are laid to Mose,
The fiendish silver-tip.

For thirty years men cursed him
When death their steers befell—
Cursed trap-marked paw and ravenous maw,
But he lived 'neath a demon spell.

As if the soul of a demon
Some pitiless, vengeful scourge,
That died while his heart for blood yet cried,
Did fierce within him surge.

From Canon town a hunter
Went forth with spirit bold;
He came no more, the years crept o'er,
And his name and fame grew old.

A dozen years—then a rider,
In a glade on a lonely height,
Found a shattered gun—men knew that one—
A shoe, and a skull bleached white.

In spring the searching herdsman
Knew well when his calves came not
By the four-toed trail through the pine-dark dale,
When he neared the gruesome spot.

Where the monster lay in waiting,
And one that went too near
Never returned—his fate unlearned,
Was guessed with dread and fear.

To the shades of Poncha mountain
Went Radcliffe forth one morn,
To hunt 'mid the crags—in gory rags—
They found him bruised and torn.

But able to tell of his seizure
By the teeth of a giant bear,
Ere he raised death's wail; the four-toed trail
Spoke the fiend that found him there.

That four-toed trail through the mountains
And its maker that defied
The tireless hound and the bullet's bound
Was spoken far and wide.

And many a knowing hunter
With trusty pack and gun
Made toilsome raids through Poncha's shades
Ere the monster's crimes were done.

At last there faithful followed
One versed in Bruin's lore—
Stout Anthony, such cunning he
Had often met before.

By Anthony that cunning
Was met and its worker fell,
And Poncha's glades and her gloomy shades
Came out of their demon spell.

Excerpted from *Outdoor Life*, January 1905

The President's Hunt

This much is common knowledge: Theodore Roosevelt was an avid hunter, he often hunted bears in Colorado, and from these trips supposedly came the infamous Teddy Bear. But the lesser-known details of Roosevelt's hunting are far more interesting: How seriously he took his writing about bears in Colorado, how race and bigotry played a role in the creation of the Teddy Bear, how his life was in danger while hunting—and not, as he probably would have preferred, from bears.

Roosevelt's first published piece of nature writing as president was an essay about one of his many Colorado bear hunts (titled, unsurprisingly, "A Colorado Bear Hunt"), in which he details the particulars of his foray deep into the Colorado mountains. Published in 1906 in *Outdoor Life* magazine, it illustrates Roosevelt's passion for hunting and his fascination with bears, perhaps because they were among the last dangerous American big game. "Bear and cougar had once been very plentiful throughout this region, but during the last three or four years the cougars have greatly diminished in numbers throughout northern Colorado," he wrote, adding that, "the bears have diminished also, although not to the same extent. The great grizzlies which were once fairly plentiful here are now very rare, as they are in most places in the United States. This Colorado trip was the first on which

I hunted bears with hounds. If we had run across a grizzly there would doubtless have been a chance to show some prowess, at least in the way of hard riding."

THE DATE was April 17, 1905. Roosevelt had completed his presidential term that began when William McKinley was assassinated, and had then been elected president on his own. On top of that, he'd just recovered from malaria and, in Europe, turmoil was increasing. It was irresponsible to go to Colorado, much less for a bear hunt, some said, but Roosevelt was insistent. He and his hunting party left Glenwood Springs, set up "Camp Roosevelt" in the high and steep mountains outside of New Castle, and proceeded with their hunt.

Despite telegrams coming in and out of camp on international affairs—particularly about the ongoing Russo-Japanese War ("I wish the Japs and Russians could settle it between themselves," Roosevelt wrote)—the president found time to wax philosophical on Colorado's scenery, calling it a "great, wild country," of which he was obviously fond: "In the creek bottoms there were a good many ranches; but we only occasionally passed by these, on our way to our hunting grounds in the wilderness along the edge of the snow-line. The mountains crowded close together in chain, peak, and tableland; all the higher ones were wrapped in an unrent shroud of snow."

Because it was April, the high mountains were still in the throes of winter and the bears were just coming out of hibernation. In the morning, Roosevelt and his hunting companion, Dr. Alexander Lambert, would ride out after breakfast. They were always accompanied by dogs—TR's fondness for dogs is legendary, and many of the photos that accompany essays about the hunt show him petting or walking with his dogs. He seems unsure about their role in the hunt, however—they admittedly made the hunt too easy, because "bears cannot, save under exceptional circumstances, escape from such a pack as we had with us." Perhaps, even, he was a bit chagrined, as when he noted, "As for the rest of us, we needed to do little more than to sit ten or twelve hours in the saddle...but it was great fun, nevertheless, and usually the chase lasted long enough to be interesting."

For several days, they went "hunting perseveringly, but unsuccessfully," but he did take time to give voice to the Colorado's other animals—the four-striped chipmunks, white-footed mice, pack-rats, woodchucks, pine squirrels, Clark's nutcrackers, and ruby-crowned kinglets that sung "with astonishing power for such tiny birds." He seemed to have loved the cold and the snow and the solitude, even if the experience did not always seem comfortable, as when he wrote: "Each day we were from six to twelve hours in the saddle, climbing with weary toil up the mountains and slipping and scrambling down them. On the tops and on the north slopes there was much snow, so that we had to pick our trails carefully, and even thus the horses often floundered belly-deep."

During his three-week foray, Roosevelt wrote of his group's switching camps because of the snow and cold, being amused by the dogs, riding over difficult terrain, running into curious locals—but above all, he seemed most interested in seeking bears.

Roosevelt's first Colorado bear kill, as he described it, was "a big male, weighing three hundred and thirty pounds." John B. Goff, who also wrote about the trip for *Outdoor Life*, comments further on the size, perhaps bragging in a way that Roosevelt cannot. Goff wrote, "Further encouragement was instilled owing to the fact that the bear was of no mean proportions, the skin after being taken off measuring seven feet six inches from nose to tip of tail and six feet six inches spread of forepaws. The President said that the hunt was a success, even if not another bear was bagged." Indeed, an-

Theodore Roosevelt, at left, near the largest black bear killed on his 1905 Colorado bear hunt.

other riding companion noted that the kill "naturally put a new life and ginger into the members of the party" and put the President "in the best of spirits."

Rather than focusing on size, Roosevelt was concerned with details of a naturalist. He wrote, "There was nothing whatever in his stomach. Evidently he had not yet begun to eat, and had been but a short while out of his hole. Bear feed very little when they first come out of their dens, sometimes beginning on grass, sometimes on buds."

As the hunt went on, more bears were brought down—several "old females" and several yearlings. One bear, which was high up in a spruce, was "a big she, with a glossy black-brown coat...I shot her through the heart...The stomach of this bear contained nothing but buds." Goff described this bear too, noting that the dogs were baying and the "President came up and, after careful aim, shot her in the neck, the bear crashing through the branches to the ground, as limp as a rag." This bear had been with a yearling—and as Roosevelt noted, when the "skin was taken off, Stewart [a hunting companion] looked at it, shook his head, and...said, 'that skin isn't big enough to use for anything but a doily.' From that time until the end of the hunt the yearlings were only known as 'doily bears.'"

But not all was well. On one evening, Roosevelt went to bed, ill, and his companions woke to find him pacing in the snow, clearly disoriented with "Cuban fever," a recurring tropical fever, which was responsible for thousands of deaths across America at the time. While Roosevelt did not admit to this in his own essay, it is well documented elsewhere, and there was clearly an alarmed fear as to his health and safety. According to records, two men led him inside, gave him lemon juice and quinine, and put him into bed. They sat with him through a very high fever and subsequent delusions.

To make matters worse, a telegram came in from Roosevelt's newly-appointed Secretary of War, William Howard Taft, about the "Russian-Japanese matter," and tensions were escalating. Roosevelt telegraphed Taft back to say he was cutting the trip short—due to his health and the increasing pressure for him to step in as mediator. And then, of course, a blizzard hit. Roosevelt described this rather calmly, noting that there "came a spell of bad weather, snowstorm and blizzard steadily succeeding one another. This lasted until my holiday was over. Some days we had to stay in camp. On other days we hunted, but there was three feet of new snow on the summits and foothills, making it difficult to get about. We saw no more bear."

According to other accounts, however, the storm was more worrisome, and his hunting party was concerned about both his health and their ability to get him out of camp. Eventually the weather improved, and the group was able to descend to Glenwood Springs—Roosevelt later recounted the return trip in typical poetic fashion: "The green of the valley was a delight to the eye; bird songs sounded on every side, from the fields and from the trees and bushes beside the brooks and... the air was sweet with the spring-time breath of many budding things."

BEARS DID NOT PROVIDE the only victory of this trip. The Colorado expedition was also a political move, and proved to be a great political stunt. As one reporter of the time noted, Roosevelt "received many visitors in camp to get a look at the President unmolested...it was hard for him to do anything else but receive them. Men came in singles, in pairs, with their boys, with the girls and with their wives. Whole families flocked in, their faces being a study of mingled curiosity and excitement. In every case, the President was most courteous and obliging." The country was beginning to fall in love with its new president, and the bear hunt only increased his presence in the public's imagination. He continued to build on the image of him as sickly child cured by his own extreme physical program, the hero of the Rough Riders, the tough man who had overcome so much.

Colorado, too, used this hunt as a tourist and publicity tool. In the introduction to the *Outdoor Life* article, J.A. McGuire wrote, "It is a fact proudly recorded by the state of Colorado that her great hunting grounds have twice been invaded by that prince of sportsmen, Theodore Roosevelt—once, three years ago, while he was vice president, and again, the past April, while President of the United States. That the president should honor the state of Colorado in so kingly a manner is a compliment to the kind and character of our big game, to our guides, to our citizens and to our great state."

This grand adventure proved to be not only a boon for Roosevelt and Colorado, but also for billions of children worldwide. Or at least, so goes one version of the many myths.

Indeed, one of the most enduring of all Rooseveltian stories is that of the Teddy Bear, the story of which is more fascinating and political than most people realize. The existence of cuddly stuffed bears, in fact, started with a political comment on racism.

In November of 1902, after arbitrating a tense Appalachian coal strike, President Theodore Roosevelt rested by going black-bear hunting in Mississippi. While some local newspapers welcomed him to their state, others sneered at Roosevelt in obscene terms, still furious because he'd hosted Booker T. Washington at dinner in the White House the previous year. The president had made his feelings about "drawing the line" against racism more than clear.

Roosevelt wanted his first black-bear trophy, and a railroad company arranged for a trip to the Mississippi Delta, where the bears were populous, and strenuously hunted.

They hired 56-year-old "bear man" Holt Collier, the area's pre-eminent guide, and they provided hunting dogs, several railroad executives as companions, and elaborate meals. Collier, a dignified former slave and self-supporting woodsman, and the president became quick friends and stayed up late swapping hunting tales.

The railroad men emphasized to Collier that the first bear had to be Roosevelt's kill, but when that animal was cornered Roosevelt was back at the base camp. While Collier bugled a signal, some men let the dogs loose on the large, mature but starving bear, and they began mauling it. Disgusted, Collier pulled the dogs off, knocked the bear unconscious and tied it to a tree for Roosevelt's arrival. But the latter refused to shoot a trussed-up animal and told others to end its misery themselves. The hunt, overall, was a bust for Roosevelt, but pro-Roosevelt newspapers played up his honorable hunter's code.

The *Washington Post* ran a cartoon by Clifford K. Berryman that made a visual pun linking the bear incident with the president's race policy. The cartoonist sketched a very black bear being roped by the neck by a white catcher, and Roosevelt turning away in disgust—a comment on racism in the South. Berryman was soon asked to do more cartoons, and with repetition, the bear became smaller, rounder, and cuter. The teddy bear, in other words, was being invented in political cartoons.

What happened next, in terms of the Teddy Bear, is the stuff of stories. While Roosevelt was in Colorado, he often stayed at Hotel Colorado, located in Glenwood Springs, and according to one legend, the teddy bear originated here. To cheer Roosevelt after an unsuccessful day of hunting, hotel maids supposedly presented him with a stuffed bear pieced together from scraps of material. Later, his daughter Alice admired it by saying, "I will call it Teddy." In any case, by

This widely reprinted 1902 drawing, by Washington Post *political cartoonist Clifford K. Berryman, changed guide Holt Collier's race and the bear's size and age, but tied together the hunt and Roosevelt's "drawing the line" on various dishonorable practices. It also led to invention of the toy Teddy Bear, and wide use of the nickname that Roosevelt and his family detested and never used.*

coincidence or not, after the Mississippi cartoons and the Colorado hunts, FAO Schwarz began making stuffed bears—and billions have been sold and dragged about on their own expeditions.

AFTER HIS Colorado trip, Roosevelt returned to Washington to attend to matters. His reputation as a hunter and an outdoorsman were secure, as charmingly put by one reporter of the day: "There are no words which could so adequately express the quality of sport to be found within our confines as the mere statement that so critical a sportsman as Theodore Roosevelt." The rest of the story, as they say, is history. In a decisive naval battle, Japan got the upper hand, which apparently brought Russia to the peace table; in 1905 a treaty was signed, ending Russia's expansionist policy in eastern Asia, and giving Japan effective control of Korea and much of Manchuria. The next year, Roosevelt won the 1906 Nobel Peace Prize (the first American to do so) for his diplomacy in the matter. He went on to finish his presidency, continued hunting, continued politics, and continued to write about the natural world, publishing over fifty volumes and hundreds of articles. Roosevelt also continued to write about bears (the best collection of his fine writings are found in *American Bears* by Paul Schullery). He clearly loved writing, storytelling, and bears, and his contributions are valuable both as literature and natural history. He died at the age of sixty, after getting sick on another trip.

I like this story, because it offers us something beyond the dog-loving, forest-creating, Rough Riding, chubby-cheeked, round-glasses guy. I also like thinking about what Colorado gave him, perhaps: the gift of solitude to prepare for one of his greatest achievements, a snowstorm and a disease to focus him, a bear to put "ginger" into his step. And he gave us something, too: The gift of his observation and language. Of his last day in Colorado, he wrote: "On the last day we rode down to where Glenwood Springs lies, hemmed in by lofty mountain chains, which are riven in sunder by sheer-sided, cliff-walled canyons. As we left ever farther behind us the wintry desolation of our high hunting grounds we rode into full spring."

A Colorado Bear Hunt

By Theodore Roosevelt

IN MID-APRIL, nineteen hundred and five, our party, consisting of Philip B. Stewart, of Colorado Springs, and Dr. Alexander Lambert, of New York, in addition to myself, left Newcastle, Col., for a bear hunt. As guides and hunt vers we had John Goff and Jake Borah, than whom there are no better men at the work of hunting bear in the mountains with hounds. Each brought his own dogs; all told, there were twenty-six hounds, and four half-blood terriers to help worry the bear when at bay. We travelled in comfort, with a big pack train, spare horses for each of us, and a cook, packers, and horse wranglers. I carried one of the new model Springfield military rifles, a 30-40, with a soft-nosed bullet—a very accurate and hard-hitting gun.

This first day we rode about twenty miles to where camp was pitched on the upper waters of East Divide Creek. It was a picturesque spot. At this altitude it was still late winter and the snow lay in drifts, even in the creek bottom, while the stream itself was not yet clear from ice. The tents were pitched in a grove of leafless aspens and great spruces, beside the rushing, ice-rimmed brook. The cook tent, with its stove, was an attractive place on the cool mornings and in stormy weather. Fry, the cook, a most competent man, had rigged up a table, and we had folding camp-chairs—luxuries utterly unknown to my former camping trips. Each day we breakfasted early and dined ten or twelve hours later, on returning from the day's hunt; and as we carried no lunch, the two meals were enjoyed with ravenous pleasure by the entire company. The horses were stout, tough, shaggy beasts, of wonderful staying power, and able to climb like cats. The country was very steep and rugged; the mountain-sides were greasy and slippery from the melting snow, while the snow bucking through the deep drifts on their tops and on the north sides was exhausting. Only sure-footed animals could avoid serious tumbles, and only animals of great endurance could have lasted through the work. Both Johnny Goff and his partner, Brick Wells, who often accompanied us on the hunts, were frequently mounted on animals of uncertain temper, with a tendency to buck on insufficient provocation; but they rode them with entire indifference up and down any incline. One of the riders, "Al," a very good tempered man, a tireless worker, had as one of his horses a queer, big-headed dun beast, with a black stripe down its back and traces of zebra-like bands on the backs of his front les. He was an atavistic animal, looking much as the horses must have looked which an age or two ago lived in this very locality and were preyed on by sabre-toothed tigers, hyenadons, and other strange and terrible beasts of a long-vanished era. Lambert remarked to him: "Al, you ought to call that horse of yours 'fossil'; he is a hundred thousand years old." To which Al, with immovable face, replied: "Gee! and that man sold him to me for a seven-year-old! I'll have the law on him!"

The hounds were most interesting, and showed all the variations of character and temper to be expected in such a pack; a pack in which performance counted for everything and pedigree for nothing. One of the best hounds was half fox terrier. Three of Johnny's had been with us four years before, when he and I hunted cougars together; these three being Jim, now an old dog, who dropped behind in a hard run, but still [was] excellent on a cold trail; Tree'em, who, like Jim, had grown aged, but was very sure; and Bruno, who had become one of the best of all the pack on a hot trail, but who was apt to overrun it if it became at all difficult and cold. The biggest dog of the pack, a very powerful animal, was Badge, who was half foxhound and half what Johnny called Siberian bloodhound—I suppose a Great Dane or Ulm dog. His full brother Bill came next to him. There was a Rowdy in Jake's pack, and another Rowdy in Johnny's, and each got badly hurt before the hunt was through. Jake's Rowdy, as soon as an animal was killed, became very cross and wished to attack any dog that came near. One of Jake's best hounds was old Bruise, a very sure, although not a particularly fast dog. All the members of the pack held the usual man-beast attitude toward one another. They joined together for the chase and the fight, but once the quarry was killed, their relations among themselves became those of active hostility or selfish indifference. At feeding time each took whatever his strength permitted, and each paid abject deference to whichever animal was his known superior in prowess. Some of the younger dogs would now and then run deer or coyote. But the older dogs paid heed only to bear and bobcat; and the pack, as a body, discriminated sharply between the hounds they could trust and those which would go off on a wrong trail. The four terriers included a heavy, liver-colored half-breed bull-dog, a preposterous animal who looked as if his ancestry had included a toadfish. He was a terrible fighter, but his unvarying attitude toward mankind was one of the effusive and rather foolish affection. In a fight he could whip any of the hounds save Badge, and he was far more willing than Badge to accept punishment. There was also a funny little black and tan, named Skip, a most friendly little fellow, especially fond of riding in front or behind the saddle of any one of us who would take him up, although perfectly able to travel forty miles a day on his own sturdy legs if he had to, and then to join in the worry of the quarry when once it had been shot. Porcupines abounded in the woods, and one or two of the terriers and half a dozen of the hounds positively refused to learn any wisdom, invariable attacking each porcupine they found; the result being that we had to spend many minutes in removing the quills from their mouths, eyes, etc. A white bull-terrier would come in from such a combat with his nose literally looking like a glorified pincushion, and many of the spines we had to take out with nippers. The terriers never ran with the hounds, but stayed behind with the horses until they heard the hounds barking "bayed" or "treed," when they forthwith tore toward them. Skip adopted me as his special master, rode with me whenever I would let him, and slept on the foot of my bed at night, growling defiance at anything that came near. I grew attached to the friendly, bright little fellow, and at the end of the hunt took him home with me as a playmate for the children.

It was a great, wild country. In the creek bottoms there were a good many ranches; but we only occasionally passed by these, on our way to our hunting grounds in the wilderness along the edge of the snow-line. The mountains crowded close together in chain, peak, and tableland; all the higher ones were wrapped in an unrent shroud of snow. We saw a good many deer, and fresh sign of elk, but no elk themselves, although we were informed that bands were to be found in the high spruce timber where the snows were so deep that it would have been impossible to go on horseback, while going on foot would have been inconceivably fatiguing. The country was open. The high peaks were bare of trees. Cottonwoods, and occasionally dwarfed birch or maple and willows, fringed the streams; aspens grew in groves higher up. There were pinyons and cedars on the slopes of the foothills; spruce clustered here and there in the cooler ravines and valleys and high up the mountains. The dense oak brush and thick growing cedars were hard on our clothes, and sometimes on our bodies.

Bear and cougars had once been very plentiful throughout this region, but during the last three or four years the cougars have greatly diminished in numbers throughout northern Colorado, and the bears have diminished also, although not to the same extent. The great grizzlies which were once fairly plentiful here are now very rare, as they are in the most places in the United States. There remain plenty of the black and brown bears, which are simply individual color phases of the same species.

This Colorado trip was the first on which I hunted bears with hounds. If we had run across a grizzly there would doubtless have been a chance to show some prowess, at least in the way of hard riding. But the black and brown bears cannot, save under exceptional circumstances, escape such a pack as we had with us; and the real merit of the chase was confined to the hounds and to Jake and Johnny for their skill in handling them. Perhaps I should add the horses, for their extraordinary endurance and surefootedness. As for the rest of us, we needed to do little more than to sit ten or twelve hours in the saddle and occasionally lead the horses up or down the most precipitous and cliff-like of the mountain sides. But it was great fun, nevertheless, and usually a chase lasted long enough to be interesting....

Next morning we rode off early, taking with us all twenty-six hounds and the four terriers. We wished first to find whether the bear had gone out of the country in which we had seen him, and so rode up a valley and then scrambled laboriously up the mountain-side to the top of the snow-covered divide. Here the snow was three feet deep in places, and the horses plunged and floundered as we worked our way in single file through the drifts. But it had frozen hard the previous night, so that a bear could walk on the crust and leave very little sign. In consequence we came near passing over the place where the animal we were after had actually crossed out of the canyon-like ravine in which we had seen him and gone over the divide into another set of valleys. That trail was so faint that it puzzled us, as we could not be certain how fresh it was and until this point could be cleared up we tried to keep the hounds from following it. Old Jim, however, slipped off to one side and speedily satisfied himself that the trail was fresh. Along it he went, giving tongue, and the other dogs were maddened by the sound, while Jim, under such circumstances, paid no heed whatever to any effort to make him come back. Accordingly, the other hounds were slipped after him, and down they ran into the valley, while we slid, floundered, and scrambled along the ridge crest parallel to them, until a couple of miles farther on we worked our way down to some great slopes covered with dwarf scrub-oak. At the edge of these slopes, where they fell off in abrupt descent to the stream at the bottom of the valley, we halted. Opposite us was a high and very rugged mountain-side covered with a growth of pinyon—never a close-growing tree—its precipitous flanks broken by ledges and scored by gullies and ravines. It was hard to follow the scent across such a mountain-side, and the dogs speedily became much scattered. We could hear them plainly, and now and then could see them, looking like ants as they ran up and down hill and along the ledges. Finally we heard some of them barking bayed. The volume of sound increased steadily as the straggling dogs joined those which had first reached the hunted animal. At about this time, to our astonishment, Badge, usually a stanch fighter, rejoined us, followed by one or two other hounds, who seemed to have had enough of the matter. Immediately afterward we saw the bear, half-way up the opposite mountainside [sic]. The hounds were all around him, and occasionally bit at his hind quarters; but he had evidently no intention of climbing a tree. When we first saw him he was sitting up on a point of rock surrounded by the pack, his black fur showing to fine advantage. Then he moved off, threatening the dogs, and making what in Mississippi is called a walking bay. He was a sullen, powerful beast, and his leisurely gait showed how little he feared the pack, and how confident he was in his own burly strength. By this time the dogs had been after him for a couple of hours, and as there was no water on the mountain-side we feared they might be getting exhausted, and rode toward them as rapidly as we could. It was a hard climb up to where they were, and we had to lead the horses. Just as we came in sight of him, across a deep gully which ran down the sheer mountain-side, he broke bay and started off, threatening the foremost of the pack as they dared to approach him. They were all around him, and for a minute I could not fire; then as he passed under a pinyon I got a clear view of his great round stern and pulled trigger. The bullet broke both his hips, and he rolled down the hill, the hounds yelling with excitement as the closed in on him. He could still play havoc with the pack, and there was need to kill him at once. I leaped and slid down on my side of the gully as he rolled down his; at the bottom he stopped and raised himself on his fore quarters [sic]; and with another bullet I broke his back between the shoulders.

Immediately all the dogs began to worry the carcass, while their savage baying echoed so loudly in the narrow, steep gully that we could with difficulty hear one another speak. It was a wild scene to look upon, as we scrambled down to where the dead bear lay on his back between the rocks. He did not die wholly unavenged, for he had killed one of the terriers and six other dogs were more or less injured. The chase of the bear is grim work for the pack. Jim, usually a very wary fighter, had a couple of deep holes in his thigh; but the most mishandled of the wounded dogs was Shorty. With his usual dauntless courage he had gone straight at the bear's head. Being such a heavy, powerful animal, I think if he had been backed up he could have held the bear's head down, and prevented the beast from doing much injury. As it was, the bear bit through the side of Shorty's head, and bit him in the shoulder, and again in the hip, inflicting very bad wounds. Once the fight was over Shorty lay down on the hillside, unable to move. When we started home we put him beside a little brook, and left a piece of bear meat by him, as it was obvious we could not get him to camp that day. Next day one of the boys went back with a pack-horse to take him in; but halfway out met him struggling toward camp, and returned. Late in the afternoon Shorty turned up while we were at dinner, and staggered toward us, wagging his tail with enthusiastic delight at seeing his friends. We fed him until he could not hold another mouthful; then he curled up in a dry corner of the cook-tent and slept for forty-eight hours; and two or three days afterward was able once more to go hunting.

The bear was a big male, weighing three hundred and thirty pounds. On examination at close quarters, his fur, which was in fine condition, was not as black as it had seemed when seen afar off, the roots of the hairs being brown. There was nothing whatever in his stomach. Evidently he had not yet begun to eat, and had been but a short while out of his hole. Bear feed very little when they first come out of their dens, sometimes beginning on grass, sometimes on buds. Occasionally they will feed at carcasses and try to kill animals within a week or two after they have left winter quarters, but this is rare, and as a usual thing for the first few weeks after they have come out they feed much as a deer would. Although not hog fat, as would probably been the case in the fall, this bear was in good condition. In the fall, however, he would doubtless have weighed over four hundred pounds. The three old females we got on this trip weighted one hundred and thirty-five pounds apiece. The yearlings weighed from thirty-one to forty pounds. The only other black bears I ever weighed all belong to the sub-species *Luteolus*, and were killed on the little Sunflower River, in Mississippi, in the late fall of nineteen hundred and two. A big old male, in poor condition, weighed two hundred and eighty-five pounds, and two very fat females weighed two hundred and twenty and two hundred and thirty-five pounds respectively.

The next few days we spent in hunting perseveringly, but unsuccessfully. Each day we were from six to twelve hours in the saddle, climbing with weary toil up the mountains and slipping and scrambling down them. On the tops and on the north slopes there was much snow, so that we had to pick our trails carefully, and even thus the horses often foundered belly-deep as we worked along in single file; the men on the horses which were best at snow bucking took turns in breaking the trail. In the worst places we had to dismount and lead the horses, often over such bad ground that nothing less sure-footed than the tough mountain ponies could even have kept their legs. The weather was cold, with occasional sharp flurries of snow, and once a regular snowstorm. We found the tracks of one or two bears, but in each case several days old, and it was evident either that the bears had gone back to their dens, finding the season so late, or else that they were lying quiet in sheltered places, and traveling as little as possible.... After a week of this we came to the conclusion that the snow was too deep and the weather too cold for us to expect to get any more bear in the immediate neighborhood, and accordingly shifted camp to where Clear Creek joins West Divide Creek.

The first day's hunt from the new camp was successful. We were absent about eleven hours and rode some forty miles. The day included four hours' steady snow bucking, for the bear, as soon as they got the chance, went through the thick timber where the snow lay deepest. Some two hours after leaving camp we found the old tracks of a she and a yearling, but it took us a much longer time before we finally struck the fresh trail made late the previous night or early in the morning. It was Jake who first found this fresh track, while Johnny with the pack was a couple of miles away, slowly but surely puzzling out the cold trail and keeping the dogs up to their work. As soon as Johnny came up we put all the hounds on the tracks, and away they went, through and over the snow, yelling their eager delight. Meanwhile we had fixed our saddles and were ready for what lay ahead. It was wholly impossible to ride at the tail of the pack, but we did our best to keep within sound of the baying. Finally after much hard work and much point riding through snow, slush, and deep mud, on the level, and along, up, and down sheer slopes, we heard the dogs barking treed in the middle of a great grove of aspens high up the mountainside. The snow was too deep for the horses, and leaving them, we trudged heavily up on foot. The yearling was in the top of a tall aspen. Lambert shot it with his rifle and we then put the dogs on the trail of the old she. Some of the young ones did not know what to make of this, evidently feeing that the tracks must be those of the bear that they had already killed; but the veterans were in fully [sic] cry at once. We scrambled after them up the steep mountain, and then downward along ridges and spurs, getting all the clear ground we could. Finally we had to take to the snow, and floundered and slid through the drifts until we were in the valley. Most of the time the dogs were within hearing, giving tongue as they followed the trail. Finally a total change in the note showed that they were barking treed; and as rapidly as possible we made out way toward the sound. Again we found ourselves unable to bring the horses up to where the bear had treed, and scrambled thither on foot through the deep snow.

The bear was some thirty or forty feet up a tall spruce; it was a big she, with a glossy black-brown coat. I was afraid that at our approach she might come down; but she had been running hard for some four hours, had been pressed close, and evidently had not the slightest idea of putting herself of her own free will within the reach of the pack, which was now frantically baying at the foot of the tree. I shot her through the heart. As the bullet struck she climbed up through the branches with great agility for six or eight feet; then her muscles relaxed, and down she came with a thud, nearly burying herself in the snow. Little Skip was one of the first dogs to seize her as she came down; and in another moment he literally disappeared under the hounds as they piled on the bear. As soon as possible we got off the skin and pushed campward at a good gait, for we were a long way off. Just at nightfall we came out on a bluff from which we could overlook the rushing, swirling brown torrent, on the farther bank of which the tents were pitched.

The stomach of this bear contained nothing but buds. Like the other shes killed on this trip, she was accompanied by her yearling young, but had no newly born cub; sometimes bear breed only every other year, but I have found the mother accompanied not only by her cub but by her young of the year before. The yearling also had nothing but buds in its stomach. When its skin was taken off, Stewart looked at it, shook his head, and turning to Lambert said solemnly, "Alex., [sic] that skin isn't big enough to use for anything but a doily." From that time until the end of the hunt the yearlings were only known as "doily bears."

Next morning we again went out, and this time for twelve

hours steadily, in the saddle, and now and then on foot. Most of the time we were in snow, and it was extraordinary that the horses could get through it at all, especially in working up the steep mountain-sides. But until it got so deep that they actually floundered—that is, so long as they could get their legs down to the bottom—I found that they could travel much faster than I could. On this day some twenty good-natured, hard-riding young fellows from the ranches within a radius of a dozen miles had joined our party to "see the President kill a bear." They were a cheerful and eagerly friendly crowd, as hardy as so many young moose, and utterly fearless horsemen; one of them rode his wild, nervous horse bareback, because it had bucked so when he tried to put the saddle on it that morning that he feared he would get left behind, and so abandoned the saddle outright. Whenever they had a chance they all rode at headlong speed, paying no heed to the slope of the mountainside [sic] or the character of the ground. In the deep snow they did me a real service, for of course they had to ride their horses single file through the drifts, and by the time my turn came we had a good trail.

After a good deal of beating to and fro, we found where an old she-bear with two yearlings had crossed a hill during the night and put the hounds on their tracks. Johnny and Jake, with one or two of the cowboys, followed the hounds over the exceedingly difficult hillside where the trail led; or rather, they tried to follow them, for the hounds speedily got clear away, as there were many places where they could run on the crust of the snow, in which the horses wallowed almost helpless. The rest of us went down to the valley, where the snow was light and the going easier. The bear had travelled hither and thither through the woods on the sidehill, and the dogs became scattered. Moreover, they jumped several deer, and four or five of the young dogs took after one of the latter. Finally, however, the rest of the pack put up the three bears. We had an interesting glimpse of the chase as the bears quartered up across an open spot of the hillside. The hounds were but a short distance behind them, strung out in a long string, the more powerful, those which could do best in the snow-bucking, taking the lead. We pushed up the mountain-side after them, horse after horse getting down in the snow, and speedily heard the redoubled clamor which told us that something had been treed. It was half an hour before we could make our way to the tree, a spruce, in which the two yearlings had taken refuge, while around the bottom the entire pack was gathered, crazy with excitement. We could not take the yearlings alive, both because we lacked the means of carrying them, and because we were anxious to get after the old bear. We could not leave them where they were, because it would have been well-nigh impossible to get the dogs away, they would not have run any other trail as long as they knew the yearlings were in the tree. It was therefore out of the question to leave them unharmed, as we should have been glad to do, and Lambert killed them both with his revolver; the one that was first hit immediately began biting its brother. The ranchmen took them home to eat.

The hounds were immediately put on the trail of the old one and disappeared over the snow. In a few minutes we followed. It was heavy work getting up the mountainside [sic] through the drifts, but once on top we made our way down a nearly bare spur, and then turned to the right, scrambled a couple of miles along a slippery sidehill, and halted, below us lay a great valley, on the farther side of which a spruce forest stretched up toward the treeless peaks. Snow covered even the bottom of the valley, and lay deep and solid in the spruce forest on the mountain-side. The hounds were in full cry, evidently on a hot trail, and we caught glimpses of them far on the opposite side of the valley, crossing little open glades in the spruce timber. If the crust was hard they scattered out.

Where it was at all soft they ran in single file. We worked our way down toward them, and on reaching the bottom of the valley, went up it as fast as the snow would allow. Finally we heard the pack again barking treed and started toward them. They had treed the bear far up the mountainside [sic] in the thick spruce timber, and a short experiment showed us that the horses could not possibly get through the snow. Accordingly, off we jumped and went toward the sound on foot, all the young ranchmen and cowboys rushing ahead, and thereby making me an easy trail. On the way to the tree the rider of the bareback horse pounced on a snowshoe rabbit which was crouched under a bush and caught it with his hands. It was half an hour before we reached the tree, a big spruce, up which the bear had gone to a height of some forty feet. I broker her neck with a single bullet. She was smaller than the one I had shot the day before, but full grown. In her stomach, as in those of the two yearlings, there were buds of rose-bushes and quaking aspens. One yearling had also swallowed a mouse. It was a long ride to camp, and darkness had fallen by the time we caught the gleam from the lighted tents, across the dark stream.

With neither of these last two bear had there been any call for prowess; my part was merely to kill the bear dead at the first shot, for the sake of the pack. But the days were very enjoyable, nevertheless. It was good fun to be twelve hours in the saddle in such wild and beautiful country, to look at and listen to the hounds as they worked, and finally to see the bear treed and looking down at the maddened pack baying beneath.

For the next two or three days I was kept in camp by a touch of Cuban fever....

Following this came a spell of bad weather, snowstorm and blizzards steadily succeeding one another. This lasted until my holiday was over. Some days we had to stay in camp. On other days we hunted; but there was three feet of new snow on the summits and foothills, making it difficult to get about. We saw no more bear, and, indeed, no more bear-tracks that were less than two or three weeks old....

On Sunday we rode down some six miles from camp to a little blue school-house and attended service. The preacher was in the habit of riding over every alternate Sunday from Rifle, a little town twenty or twenty-five miles away; and the ranchmen with their wives and children, some on horseback, some in wagons, had gathered from thirty miles round [sic] to attend the service. The crowd was so large that the exercises had to take place in the open air, and it was pleasant to look at the strong frames and rugged, weather-beaten faces of the men; while as for the women, one respected them even more than the men.

In spite of the snowstorms spring was coming; some of the trees were beginning to bud and show green, more and more flowers were in bloom, and bird life was steadily increasing. In the bushes by the streams the handsome white-crowned sparrows and green-tailed towhees were in full song, making attractive music; although the song of neither can rightly be compared in point of plaintive beauty with that of the white-throated sparrow, which, except some of the thrushes, and perhaps the winter wren, is the sweetest singer of the Northwestern forests. The spurred towhees were very plentiful; and one morning a willow-thrush sang among the willows like a veery. Both the crested jays and the Woodhouse jays came around camp. Lower down the Western [sic] meadow larks were singing beautifully, and vesper finches were abundant. Say's flycatcher, a very attractive bird, with pretty, soft-colored plumage, continually uttering a plaintive single note, and sometimes a warbling twitter, flitted about in the neighborhood of the little log ranch houses. Gangs of blackbirds visited the corrals. I saw but one song sparrow, and curiously enough, though I think it was merely an individual peculiarity, this particular bird had a song entirely different from any I have heard from the familiar Eastern [sic] bird—always a favorite of mine.

While up in the mountains hunting, we twice came upon owls, which were rearing their families in the deserted nests of the red-tailed hawk. One was a long-eared owl, and the other a great horned owl, of the pale Western variety. Both were astonishingly tame, and we found it difficult to make them leave their nests, which were in the tops of cottonwood trees.

On the last day we rode down to where Glenwood Springs lies, hemmed in by lofty mountain chains, which are riven in sunder by sheer-sided, cliff-walled canyons. As we left ever farther behind us the wintry desolation of our high hunting grounds we rode into full spring. The green of the valley was a delight to the eye; bird songs sounded one very side, from the fields and from the trees and bushes beside the brooks and irrigation ditches; the air was sweet with the spring-time breath of many budding things. The sarvice [sic] bushes were white with bloom, like shad-blow on the Hudson; the blossoms of the Oregon grape made yellow mats on the ground. We saw the chunky Say's ground squirrel, looking like a big chipmunk, with on each side a conspicuous white stripe edged with black. In one place we saw quite a large squirrel, grayish, with red on the lower back. I suppose it was only a pine squirrel, but it looked like one of the gray squirrels of southern Colorado. Mountain mockers and the handsome, bold Arkansaw [sic] king birds were numerous. The blacktail sage sparrow was conspicuous in the sagebrush, and high among the cliffs the white-throated swifts were soaring. There were numerous warblers, among which I could only make out the black-throated gray, Audubon's, and McGillivray's. In Glenwood Springs itself the purple finches, house finches, and

Bullock's orioles were in full song. Flocks of siskins passed with dipping flight. In one rapid little stream we saw a water ousel. Hummingbirds—I supposed the broad-tailed—were common, and as they flew they made, intermittently, and almost rhythmically, a curious metallic sound; seemingly it was done with their wings.

But the thing that interested me most of the way of bird life was something I saw in Denver. To my delight I found that the huge hotel at which we took dinner was monopolized by the pretty, musical house finches, to the exclusion of the ordinary city sparrows. The latter are all too plentiful in Denver, as in every other city, and, as always, are noisy, quarrelsome—in short thoroughly unattractive and disreputable. The house finch, on the contrary, is attractive in looks, in song, and in ways. It was delightful to hear the males singing, often on the wing. They went right up to the top stories of the high hotel, and nested under the eaves and in the cornices. The cities of the Southwestern states are to be congratulated on having this spirited, attractive little songster as a familiar dweller around their houses and in their gardens.

Excerpted from *Outdoor Pastimes of an American Hunter*, by Theodore Roosevelt. New York: Charles Scribner's Sons, 1905.

THE BEST HISTORICAL NEWSPAPER STORIES

OLD NEWSPAPER accounts are nutty. Call me crazy, but I've always loved 'em for that reason—the odd spelling, the great typesetting (and typesetting mistakes), the charm of that day and age. It was with good humor, then, that I went through Colorado's earliest newspapers looking for bear stories. Admittedly, many are simply accounts along the lines of "so-and so-encountered a bear"—not all that interesting, really. Some stories, however, offer exquisite glimpses into the life and times of early Coloradoans, or of bears.

Here I offer the best stories I could find from around the state—some funny, some sad, some a hard look at hard times. In order to accurately illustrate the times, these stories are included with their original spelling and sentence structure (the headlines, in particular, are often endearing). The articles are presented in chronological order. In some cases, the type was illegible or missing, and in some cases, I opted to shorten long accounts. More or less, however, here are the original and verbatim earliest printed accounts of bears in Colorado.

[Pitkin County] *Rocky Mountain Sun*, August 18, 1883
LYNCHERS FOILED BY A BEAR
A Colorado man, who expected a gang of lynchers to come for him about the middle of the night, took himself to the cel-

lar, leaving a pet grizzly bear in his place in bed. The lynchers didn't bring any lights but made a very plucky attempt to get the bear out and lynch it, but gave it up after three of them had lost an eye apiece, two had suffered the loss of thumbs, chewed off, and the other six were more or less deprived of skin. That man now has a tremendous reputation as a fighter and the bear didn't mind the work one bit.

[Pitkin County] *Rocky Mountain Sun,* June 21, 1884
TRAPPING A GRIZZLY.
Trapping a grizzly has its perils and excitement also. It is quite an art to set and place a trap cunningly, and trappers vary in their methods and are wary of explaining them. I will then pass this branch of the subject. Let us suppose, therefore, that the hunter has made his camp in a neighborhood redolent of grizzlies, and that he has his traps set in a likely place for a bear...It may be accepted as a maxim that a grizzly will eventually get loose, and ordinarily in a few hours...When you have trapped a thousand-pound grizzly, you have not caught a bear; you have simply caught the devil incarnate!

Fort Collins Courier, December 18, 1884
A BEAR WITH A HISTORY
One of the largest bears ever killed in Colorado is now to be seen at the meat market of Chamberlain & Alcher at Arapahoe and Sixteenth streets. It is a monster grizzly, weighing 600 pounds, and was killed a few days ago in the North Park by a hunger [sic] Sterling Ish. The animal was alone when discovered in his retreat, and at once showed fight. Ish took to his heels, and ran for dear life, but the bear was the fleetest, and after a wild chase overtook the fleeing Nimrod. Just as the bear was upon him, Ish dashed suddenly to the right, and the bear clumsily passed by in his vain endeavor to also turn at a right angle. The bear turned a few yards away, and as the mon-

ster did so, Ish, who had his rifle leveled, sent a bullet into his breast...The hunter was about to take to his heels again when he had the great satisfaction of seeing the bear slackening his speed and tottering on his feet. He ran a few yards further and then fell dead. The wound in the breast having done its work.

Yesterday the bear was viewed by hundreds of persons. It will be kept on exhibition until after the holidays.

Livingston Post, November 6, 1890
CHEWED BY A GRIZZLY

Mr. Best, of Durango, came very near losing his life recently by being devoured by a ferocious bear, and his escape is probably the most miraculous that ever occurred in the history of the state, says the *Denver Republican.*

Mr. Best was up Lightner creek looking for horses and was coming down the side of a steep canyon about 10 miles from town, and as he drew near a portion of the trail where the brush an[d] It was missing in original undergrowth was very thick he heard a crackling and smashing of the scrub o[a]k on one side.

Suddenly a low growl met his ear, and without further warning the brush parted and Mr. Best was confronted by a large, ugly-looking silvertip or range bear, that stood hardly two feet away. For a moment bruin stood as if considering what...tactics to pursue. Then raising herself upon her hind feet and waving her paw in the air, she rushed for Mr. Best, who totally unarmed, knew not how to escape the infuriated animal.

As she approached closer and closer until he could feel her hot breath in his face, he managed to catch her by the feet and being possessed on ordinary occasions of enormous strength, which now in this exciting moment became superhuman, he hel[d] her feet in such manner that she was unable, although trying her best, to strike, or tear him with her claws.

For a moment both paused for wind and Mr. Best was looking for some way to let go, but no way was found. The bear, finding herself powerless to crush her victim, as he had held her feet so widely apart that she could do nothing with them, saw her way clear to end Mr. Best's career by eating his head and face, which as both his hands were employed in holding her feet, she could do and he could not prevent it unless he should turn her feet loose, and then she would have more advantage than before.

Slowly she leaned her ugly face toward him and then opened her enormous mouth and took Best's head inside and leisur[e]ly began to crush in his head and his face with her teeth. Mr. Best was, of course, unable to stop her, and was compelled to let her pursue her man-eating course.

Finally, overcome with pain and loss of blood, Mr. Best fell backward, the bear falling on top, and being now so weak that he could offer no further resistance, bruin, finding herself free, proceeded to tear and lacerate Mr. Best's face and scalp.

While she was inflicting her punishment upon him she heard, as well as did her victim, who had not yet lost consciousness, a lot of noise from the brush, accompanied by a few sharp growls, which evidently came from her cubs. Leaving Mr. Best, she started to investigate the trouble there and disappeared.

Mr. Best, half unconscious and blinded by the blood that was flowing from the many wounds that had been inflicted on his face and head, was unable to rise, but turned over on his face and tried to think what to do.

Just as he had determined to try and find his way to some ranch or camp he heard the bushes crash and knew that the bear was returning.

Having heard that they will not bit or touch anything they think dead, he resolved to find out, and as the bear approached again he kept perfectly still Bruin came up and waited for him to jump or move, and seeing that he did not she bit him on the arm, and then finding he did not move, she nosed him a little, and after a few farewell but[t]s grunted to her cubs and plunged into the brush.

Mr. Best succeeded in dragging himself to a tie ranch five miles distant and medical assistance was summoned The physician f[o]und the man in critical condition and his recovery is still uncertain.

Aspen Daily Chronicle, June 9, 1891
ENTRAPPING A BIG BEAR

An interesting bear story, thoroughly reliable in every detail, was given to a TIMES reporter yesterday by a gentleman who come in from the scene of the incident at Robert Reed's lumber camp, located about three miles from the North Fork switch on Frying Pan. Bears have been reported to be very numerous in that vicinity this spring and so many fresh signs of their presence have been discovered lately, that a number of workmen at the camp have thrown up their positions rather than risk the danger of becoming food for these savage wild beasts. A strong, heavy trap was finally set for bruin and one morning last week when the trap was visited a monster she bear was found with one of its forearms firmly held by the teeth of the steel trap. Three little cubs were close by, and the ferocious animal was in a terrific rage. The trap was chained to a stick of timer seven or eight fee[t] long that weighed probably 100 pounds. The savage bear stood on his hind feet and hurled the stick of timber about, much as a man handles a flail. The men were actually terror-stricken by the fearful exhibition of strength and madness they witnessed. Returning to the boarding house they reported the incident, but no one seemed willing to go back and shoot the infuriated animal. The woman cook of the house, however, showed more spunk than any of them and she led the way back to the bear, and nerved Henry Sweinhart, a workman of the camp, to fire balls into the beast until it was killed. Sweinhart in his excitement swallowed a big chew of tobacco and became deathly sick.

One of the cubs were killed, but the other two, cute little rascals about a foot high, were captured. The mother bear is a beautiful specimen of the silver tipped species and weighed 400 pounds. The hide is said to be worth $60.

Aspen Tribune, November 19, 1896
The Bear and Man
Fierce Battle With a Bruin in the Ashcroft Hills
Fought to the Death
A Min[e]r Named Anderson
Had a Terrible Experience
and Was Nearly Killed.

A story came from Ashcroft yesterday to the effect that a prospector named Anderson who is working on a claim near the Tam O'Shanter group of mines, fought a terrific battle with a large black bear late last Sunday afternoon. Anderson came out victor, but it was a painful victory an he will bear some of the marks of the engagement with him to the grave.

Anderson started out early in the afternoon with a dog and Winchester rifle to hunt, bear tracks having been reported within a few miles of the mines. He and the dog picked up the track[s] and trailed them for about three miles when they became fresher and the dog bayed the fact that he had the scent. The snow [w]as quite deep and Anderson plunged through taking little or no precaution to see where he was going. He was suddenly arrested by a howl of pain from the dog and looked up only to be confronted by an enormous bear that had swatted the canine one and sent it howling toward its master. The bear squatted on its haunches waiting for Anderson to open the fight.

The man recovered from his astonishment quickly and

raising his rifle fired at random and started to retreat. In doing so his foo[t] caught in some brush and he fell. Bruin who had been hit maddened at the pain was over the prostrate man in a instant and then came a life and death struggle. Man and bear rolled over and over[.] The dog proved a valuable ally to Anderson and worried bruin considerably by biting its hind legs. So aggravating did the dog become that the bear turned its attention from the man to its tormentor. It was a fatal movement for the bear as it gave Anderson an opportunity to get out a hunting knife he carried and when bruin turned [a]gain the man closed in with the animal and buried the knife in its breast. Bruin fell over dead and Anderson dropped exhausted. The man's clothing was literally torn from him and hung in shreds. His face head body hand arm and legs were terribly lacerated and it will be several weeks before he will be able to hunt bears again.

Aspen Daily Times, July 20, 1900
KILLED A GRIZZLY.
Bear Attacks Two Cowboys
Near Collibran, Mesa County.

The following regarding an exciting fight with a grizzly bear is from the Grand Junction Sentin[e]l.

M.J. Porter and Read Markis, both of the M. J. Porter Cattle company, had an exciting experience with a large grizzly bear a few days ago that resulted in the death of bruin and the wounding of a thoroughbred horse ridden by Porter.

Porter and Martin were coming to this place from their camp on Buzzard creek, about fifteen miles northeast of here, and as they emerged from a patch of undergrowth a low grow reached their ears.

Only a short distance ahead they saw a huge grizzly directly in their path. The horses became almost uncontrollable and with only a six-shooter as a weapon of defense they decided to ride quietly around the bear and leave it captain of the field. But as they turned to leave the bear started toward them at a rapid rate.

As the trail was narrow and steep the boys decided they must either dismount and try to get away on foot or defend themselves the best way possible.

Drawing his six-shooter Markis sent a bullet into the bear's shoulder, only to increase its rage. Bruin lunged forward and struck the nearest horse, tearing the flesh from its hams in a horrible manner.

Markis threw his rope at the bear's head just as it made another lunge at Porter, and succeeded in catching it around the neck.

Throwing his gun to Porter he told him to ride as close to it as possible and shoot it between the eyes, while he attracted its attention spurring his horse. Marki[s] rushed past the bear and giving the rope a quick jerk, pulled the bear's head to one side and Porter, riding near as possible, shot it three times in the forehead in quick succession.

One of the shots had proved fatal as the bear fell forward and died in a few minutes.

The animal was male and unusually large. Markis, who is an old bear hunter, says he can't imagine what caused the bear to turn on them as it did. It was the only one he ever saw that would show fight without being cornered.

The excitement was quite novel to Porter as it was the first wild bear he had ever seen. His horse, which was a fine animal, will be crippled for life.

(Steamboat Springs) *Routt County Sentinel* September 6, 1901

GROVER CLEVELAND WILL HUNT BEAR IN COLORADO THIS FALL SO NEWSPAPER REPORTS SAY.

The Denver Republican says: Grover Cleveland, twice president of the United States, will this fall don his hunting garb and invade the wilds of Colorado in search for bear. George Newton, superintendent of Glen Beulah park, the great game preserve of the Western slope, which was a favorite hunting ground of the late Gov. Tanner of Illinois, has received a letter from John E. Wright of Chicago saying that he will visit Colorado this year on a hunting expedition and will bring the lone fisherman of Buzzard's Bay with him. Mr. Wright was in Colorado last year and shot several bear at Glen Beulah Park.

"I hope you will be able to save us a bear or two," the letter reads. "for my success of last year has inflamed the sporting blood of the ex-president and it is only through the positive assurance that I will be able to procure him a bear that I have induce him to consent to the trip."

No mention is given in the letter of the time at which the party will arrive but it is presumed it will be this month.

The advent of the late president into the hunting fields of Colorado will mark his advent into a branch of sport which he has hitherto neglected.

It is said that of late the ex-president has inclined to embonpoint [fleshiness] and has been advised that vigorous exercise is necessary to keep him from becoming stout. The doctors have told him that a daily sprint through the underbrush with a bear, in which it is fair to presume the ex president will lead, will reduce his weight rapidly. As there are other things in which Mr. Cleveland is more accomplished than in foot racing however, it is probable that he will insist that the bear shall be handicapped.

[Yuma County] *Wray Rattler* June 27, 1902
BESIEGED BY BEARS.
Colorado & Southern Telegraph Operator Wires for Help.

Denver, June 21.—"Help. Help," ticked the receiver on the desk of the dispatcher of the South Park division of the Colorado & Southern at the Union Depot Thursday night. "We are besieged by bears," went on the message. "Order out a train from Buena Vista and drive them off. I am afraid they will break into my office."

The message was sent by Operator Miller at Alpine Tunnel and he went on to explain that three bears, two large ones and a cub, had laid siege to his office. He was without firearms and feared that they would break in the doors, against which they had leaned heavily several times. The dispatcher directed the conductor of the night freight to secure a rifle along the road and be ready for carnage when he reached the eastern end of the tunnel.

The bear family remained ab[o]ut the depot for some time, sniffing at the crack in the door, and finally the operator opened an upper window and emptied a jar of vitriol upon the head of the largest one. That seemed to satisfy the bear's curiosity and it departed up the range, followed by the rest of the family. Every operator on the line was listening, and there was general relief when he announced that the siege had been raised. The armed train got in about an hour late.

Mancos Times, June 16, 1905
BIG BEAR HUNT

Steve Elkins and J.C. Sipe and wife returned from a big bear hunt Tuesday and reports [sic] six big bears from their 10 days' outing. It sees that "Teddy" and his bunch are not in it when it comes to bear hunting. Then [sic] bear were killed by the president's entire party during their month's stay in

Colorado and here our hunter accompanied by a man and his wife, with only 13 dogs killed six in ten days. The next time The President wants to take a little hunt in Colorado he had better come to Mancos and go hunting with a bear hunter if he wants to have the best luck, and a jolly good time.

Fort Collins Weekly Courier, September 5, 1906
BEARS KILL CATTLE IN THE MOUNTAINS

Bears are becoming so thick and bold in the Upper Poudre Country that people in that section are alarmed for the safety of their live stock. John Deaver, who is running cattle in company with E.R. Thayer of Greeley[,] writes his son-in-law, Harry Schreck, that these predatory creatures have already killed 40 head of young cattle in that vicinity and that scarcely a day passes that bears do not make incursions among the cattle and carry off one or more calves or yearlings for their own larder.

Campers along the river have been notified to guard well their tents and property and keep their children within hearing at all times. It is early in the season for bears to begin making inroads on the herds, as they do not usually attack cattle until later after the berry crop is exhausted. The settlers in the hills are about to organize a combined bear hunting expedition and clean out the bruin family as a means of saving their stock.

Fairplay Flume, August 30, 1907
WOMAN FRIGHTENS BEAR.

With Roman candles Mrs. Mary Moore kept off a big grizzly bear a few nights ago.

Mrs. Moore is proving on a homestead back of Cheyenne mountain. It has been her custom to barricade her cabin door at night with chairs and boxes. When a bear tried to crawl through a chink in the log hut Mrs. Moore was awakened by falling boxes. She set off the Roman candles and held them in close proximity to the animal's nose, with the result that the bear took to the timber.

Aspen Daily Times, October 22, 1908
KILLS BIG BLACK BEAR
IN HAND TO HAND FIGHT

Colorado Springs—Gene Richards, chief clerk in the Cripple Creek Short line offices here, has returned from the White river country, where he had a hand-to-hand encounter with a big black bear.

Richards had shot a fine buck, and as he approached the fallen deer, was confronted by the bear.

He shot the animal, which fell to the ground. Richards rushed up excited, only to find that bruin was only badly wounded. In his excitement he had dropped his rifle a score of yards away, and was obliged to finish the bear with his hunting knife. Richards' hands were badly scratched by the bear's claws.

Bayfield Blade, June 26 1914
TWO BEARS FIGHT TO DEATH
HUGE GRIZZLY AND A BLACK MEMBER OF BRUIN
FAMILY BATTLE TO FINISH IN DENVER PARK.

A huge male "grizzly" and a black bear cub fought a finish fight at City Park zoo. The black bear, one of a den of five, is dead. Cur[i]osity and the stimulus of a crisp spring morning are responsible.

The bear went in quest of adventure. He sniffed the air, shook himself and placed a paw upon the first crosspiece of the iron grating which separated his pen from the one adjoining, in which the grizzly, the largest in the zoo, was confined.

The visiting Bruin looked inquisitively toward the top and then commenced to mount, stopping at every round to regard inquiringly the four black bears which he had left below. From the other side of the grating the grizzly regarded the approach with disapproval.

The bear reached the top and paused to take account of his exploit with conscious satisfaction. Then he lost his balance and a moment later fell to the cement floor of the grizzly's preserve.

When the keepers arrived later the black bear was dead.

The Literary Digest, April 26, 1919
BEGINNER'S LUCK

The astounding feat of big-game hunting related in *The Oregon Journal* (Portland) as a youthful exploit of A. Phimister Procter, the sculptor, could have been performed only by a boy. No man would have dared tackle it. The future sculptor was then a slight youth of sixteen and small for his age. The episode, as told to Fred Lockley, of the Portland paper, took place in Colorado when that State was young and more of a wilderness than it is to-day. Young Procter was camping with his father and elder brother in one of the wildest and most inaccessible sections. Being considered too young to do any real hunting, it had not been thought necessary to furnish the boy with a gun of his own, but he had picked up a decrepit old 50-70 Winchester which had once been thrown away as having outworn its usefulness. Boylike, he tinkered up this weapon and finally got it to where he could sight and fire it, but the ejector refused to work. He hit upon the happy expedient of putting a 30-caliber bullet into the barrel of the gun after firing, and thus, by shaking it up and down vigorously, jarring out the empty shell[.] One day the brother and a companion had planned to make an extensive trip into the mountains to hunt big game. The younger brother was exceedingly anxious to accompany them, but was told in that tolerant and irritating way in which elder brothers sometimes speak to their juniors, that it was out of the question: that they were going on a long and dangerous expedition and could not be bothered with little boys. What happened after that is thus set forth:

It was a wonderful day for hunting big game, as there was just enough soft snow on the ground for tracking. I stuck around camp till nine o'clock and the longer I waited the more rebellious I felt at being left and told that I was too young to go along.

Finally I filled my pockets with cartridges and decided to strike [o]ut by myself and see if I could get a deer or an elk. I walked back into the hills for several hours without seeing anything. In the afternoon, somewhere about three o'clock I decided to call it a day and go back to camp. I was sitting on a fallen tree taking a rest after my long jaunt when I heard something walking leisurely through the brush near by. In an instant I was alert. A moment or so later a herd of elk walked out in the clearing. I can't begin to tell you the thrill I felt as I sat there and watched these elk walk across the hillside, utterly unconscious of my presence. In the lead was a splendid bull elk. He had magnificent antlers. Ever since I was five I had been sketching, and he appealed to my artistic sense as well as to the hunting instinct in me. I took careful aim but jut as I fired he took alarm and leapt. Instead of hitting him just back of the foreleg I broke a hind leg. There was a crash as the elk bounded away. I forgot my weariness and the fact that I was hungry , and ran after them. I had no difficulty in following the trail of blood on the snow. The rest of the herd had taken a different direction from that of the wounded leader.

Presently I came upon the wounded bull, lying down,. I ran up to cut his throat, but he had a different idea about the matter. The minute he caught sight of me he struggled to his feet and charged....I saw a large uprooted tree and scurried beneath its upturned roots. The elk tried to paw me or get at me with his horns, and [he] didn't miss me far.

My hands were trembling so I could hardly get my 38-caliber bullet out of my pocket, but I managed to drop it down the barrel of my Winchester and shake it up and down till the empty shell was ejected. I threw in another shell, and putting the muzzle of my gun between the roots I prest it against the elk's throat and fired. He fell in a heap an kicked for a minute or so, and then lay still.

I crawled out, a very shaken but proud small boy. I wanted to take that had b[u]ck to camp. It took me nearly till dusk to cut the head off at the shoulders. I swing it over my back, holding it by the prongs of the antlers. I was small and tired. It weighed nearly one hundred pounds. I started for camp, which was nearly four miles away. I would carry it a while and then sit down and rest. It was just about all I could do to stagger along with it.

...The adventures the boy had already gone throug[h] would have been considered about enough for one day by almost any adult person. Not so with this youthful Nimrod, however. Even wilder and more hair-raising experiences were in store for him. The account continues.

While I was in the ravine, dreading to tackle the job of walking back to camp, I heard a peculiar shuffling sound not far away. I wondered what it was, an[d] decided to investigate. I crawled out of the ravine, and not far away was the biggest thing on four legs I had ever seen. It was a huge grizzly bear. It was turning rotten logs an stones over to eat the [grubs] under them....With my crippled back an[d] my crippled gun I decided that if I was going to kill it I had better do the job with the first shot. Think of the folly and audacity of a boy with a defective gun starting trouble with a grizzly bear. It never occurred to me not to try not kill him.....I waited till the bear was broadside on, and then fired. He gave a roar that seemed to shake the ground. He turned his head around and began biting himself savagely where the bullet had hit him....I shot again, but this time he saw the smoke from my gun and charged. I tried my ejector. It worked, and threw out the empty shell. I got in another shot, and again he stopt and roared savagely while he bit the place where I had hit him,... he kept on coming, and I thought it was all off with me....I... fired when he was only a few yards from me. He went down, tried to get up, but couldn't make it, and began tearing the ground up with his powerful forepaws. Pretty soon he was struggling less and less, and finally he lay still.

I struck out for camp, as it was getting dark. I was about all in when I finally caught sight of our camp-fire. I walked into the light from the napping pine boughs and my father caught sight of me. He said kindly "Well, son, what luck?" I said: "Pretty fair; I killed a bull elk and a grizzly." They wouldn't believe me at first. I told them that after I had eaten supper I would guide them to the place so they could bring in the meat. My father and brother, Judge Wescott, and Ante[l]ope Jack got up the pack-horses while I was eating, and saddled them, and we struck out to where I had left the body of the bull elk. We cut him up and loaded him on the pack-horses, and then went to where I had left the elk head in the ravine where I had fallen. We found it safe and sound and the grizzly near the edge of the ravine. I had fired at it five time and hit it four time[s]. I still have one of the claws of my first grizzly.

I have hunted all over the country, both in my own country and in the Canadian Rockies and the Selkirks. I have bagged big-horn (sheep) and mountain goats, elk and grizzly, cougar and deer, but I never felt so proud as I did that night when I came in and reported I had got an elk and a grizzly. My brother and Wild Horse Jackson had been out all day and hadn't got a thing which helped take the sting from their remark about me being too young and inexperienced to go hunting with grown men.

Fort Collins Courier, July 3, 1919
BEAR UP THE POUDRE FRIGHTENS PICNICKERS
A party of picnickers from this city encountered a bear yesterday near Picnic Rock up the Poudre. They did not hesitate and give battle but jumped into their automobile and hurried home at a rapid rate of speed. In their hurry to get away they left some blankets and other articles and these may be obtained at the Northern garage.

Frank Miller and a few friends went to Picnic Rock for a few hours outing. A pet bear was taken along and given an opportunity to enjoy the scenery. The animal evidently disturbed the picnic party referred to above. The young bear enjoyed its outing but when Miller started home and made moves as tho the bear were to be left in the mountains the animal showed a disposition adverse to such plans and with remarkable speed caught the auto and climbed into the back seat.

Last week Miller took the bear to Laramie City where the animal enjoyed the Ferris wheel, merry go round and other amusements, acting like a boy at a county fair.

Fort Collins Courier, Oct. 17, 1921
THREE BLACK BEAR ARE BROT IN BY AULT MEN
"We weren't loaded for bear but we got them," declared Ivan Bader of Ault Saturday night, when he arrived in Fort Collins with the bodies of three black bears and a coyotte. He was accompanied by Frank Blow and Roy Henderson, also of Ault, the party having come in a battered Ford car, which was well loaded down. They were obliged to spend the night here to get their machine repaired.

The bears were shot by Bader and Blow in the Cameron pass district, about 130 miles northwest of Fort Collins. A she-bear weighing about 225 pounds was shot first early Wednesday morning. She ran for her den after being wounded and after trailing her a quarter of a mile, the hunters came upon the two cubs, which were also killed. The men were hunting deer but were unsuccessful in that line. They carried a .32 special Winchester and two .30-30 guns.

An[y] number of bears have been killed during the past week it is reported. A party from Estes park, including Frank Grubb and O.O. Rice of Loveland, were successful in bagging a bear it is said, while several others have reported that they have seen parties in the hills who had killed bears the black bear, while young, is not particularly vicious but a she-bear is liable to attack a man, especially if he happens to get near her den.

The bears killed by the Ault men were in prime condition.

(Telluride) *Daily Journal*, May 26, 1922
BEAR HUNTERS WANTED

Bear hunters have been invited to try out their skill on a black bear that is killing young goats on the Stearns ranch south of here. All efforts to capture or kill the bear have failed so far, according to reports from the ranch.

Chaffee County Republican, January 18, 1924
BEAR TRACKS EAT APPLES

Feeding apples to bear tracks is a new method of keeping the bear from grabbing and eating one who happens to see bear track leisurely ambling along the mountain side.

The above is a new method worked out, through deep study of the idiosyncrasies of the bruin tribe of quadrupeds that roam at will over the rugged sides of Free Gold hill by the authority on wild animal life, Mrs. A.J. Pelta.

Apples having been stored in a cellar for some time are, she says, far better for the purpose mentioned above, than fr[e]sh ones just cut from the vine.

To prove her theory she took her daughter over on the hill

a few days ago, and coming to the bear tracks, placed an apple near the tracks, and going off some distance, watch, with bated breath, the results.

Only a few golden seconds had dropped into the watershed of time, when a blood curdling scream rent through the rarified air, and then all was still except the moaning pines through which the gentle winter winds were passing—and the hungry coyote again yelped in the distance—and the ladies do not to this day know whether or not the apple was devoured by bear tracks.

THE JOURNAL OF A TRAPPER

FINDING EARLY accounts of trappers' encounters with bears isn't as easy as it sounds. Trappers, as a whole, aren't known for massive literary production, and they didn't often stop to take the time to write about bears, other than to say they ran across one, and either avoided it or shot it. And if you're looking for Colorado-only bear-trapper stories, the search gets even harder.

One exception was Osborne Russell, who wrote *Journal of a Trapper: In the Rocky Mountains Between 1834 and 1843*. This book is, in the words of its editor, Aubrey L. Haines, "perhaps the best account of the fur trapper in the Rocky Mountains when the trade there was at its peak. It is a factual, unembellished narrative written by one who was not only a trapper but also a keen observer and an able writer." Though Russell roamed across the Midwest and West, he spent much time in what would become Colorado. This excerpt is the best material on bears from a trapper that I could locate (complete with all his spelling and grammar).

April 29, 1837
   The next morning we made another start as formerly. My intentions were to set my traps on Rocky fork which we reached about 3 oclk P.M. our party having diminished

to three men beside myself. In the meanwhile it began to rain and we Stopped to approach a band of Buffaloe and as myself and one of My conrades (a Canadian) were walking along half bent near some bushes secreting ourselves from the Buffaloe a large Grizzly Bear who probably had been awakened from his slumbers by our approach sprang upon the Canadian who was 5 or 6 feet before me and placing one forepaw upon his head and the other on his left shoulder pushed him one side about 12 ft. with as little ceremony as if he had been a cat sill keeping a direct course as tho. Nothing had happened. I called to the Cannadian and soon found the fright exceeded the wound as he had received no injury except what this impudent stranger had done by tearing his coat but it was hard telling which was the most frightened the man or the Bear. We reached Rocky fork about Sunset an[d] going along [t]he edge of [t]he timber saw another Bear lying with a Buffaloe Calf lying between his forepaws which he had already killed while the Mother was standing about 20 paces distant Moaning very pitifully for the loss of her young. The bear on seeing us dropped the calf & took to his heels into the brush.

Later that year, Russell writes:

The trappers often remarked to each other as they rode over these lonely plains that it was time for the White man to leave the mountains as Beaver and game had nearly disappeared On the 15th of Novr I started up a high mountain in search of sheep after hunting and scrambling over the rocks for half the day without seeing any traces of them[.] I sat down upon a rock which overlooked the county below me at length[. C]asting a glance along the South side of the Mountain I discovered a large Grizzly bear stiting at the mouth of its den I approached within about 180 paces shot and missed it. he looked round and crept slowly into his den I reloaded my rifle went up to the hole and threw done a stone weighing 5 or 6 lbs which soon rattled to the bottom and I heard no more I then rolled a stone weighing 3 or 400 lbs into the den stepped back and prepared myself for the out come. The Stone had scarcely reached the bottom when the Bear came rushng out with his mouth wide open and was on the point of making a spring at me when I pulled the trigger and Shot him thro the left shoulder which sent him rolling down the Mountain.

At the end of his journal, Russell writes that "It has been my design whilst Keeping a journal to note down the principal circumstances which came under my immediate observation as I passed along and I have mostly deferred giving a general description of Indians and animals that inhabit the Rocky Mountains." Then, filling in that blank, Russell offers his observations about many animals, including bears:

THE GRIZZLY BEAR

Much has been said by travellers in regard to this animal yet while giving a description of animals that inhabit the Rocky Mountains I do not feel justified in silently passing over in silence [t]he most ferocious species without endeavoring to contribute some little information respecting it which altho it may not be important I hope some of it at least will be new. It lives chiefly upon roots and berries being of too slow a nature to live much upon game of its own killing and from May to Septr. It never tastes flesh. The rutting season is in Novr. and the Female brings forth from 1 to 3 at a birth[.] I have not been able to ascertan the precise time that the female goes with young but I suppose from experience and enquiry it is about 14 weeks. The young are untamable and manifest a savage ferocity when scarcely old enough to crawl. Several experiments have been tried in the Rocky Mountain for taming them but to no effect. They are possessed with great muscular strength[;] I have seen a female which was wounded by a rifle ball in the loins so as to disable her kill her young with one stroke of the fore paw as fast as they approached her. If a young Cub is wounded and commences making a noise the mother immediately springs upon it and kills it when grown they never make a noise except a fearful growl they get to be fatter than any other animals in the Rocky Mts during the season when wild fruit is abundant. The flesh of the Grizzly Bear is preferable to Pork—It lives in winter in caves in the Rocks or holes dug in the ground on high Ridges[.] It loses no flesh while confined to its den in the winter but is equally as fat in the Spring when it leaves the den as when it enters it at the beginning of the winter. There is seldom to be found more than one in the den excepting the female and her young. I have seen them measure seven feet from the tip of the nose to the insertion of the tail. It will generally run from the scent of a man but when it does not get the scent it will often let him approach close enough to spring upon him and when wounded it is a dangerous animal to trifle with. Its speed is comparatively slow down hill but much greater in ascending it never climbs trees as its claws are too straight for that purpose.

THE BLACK BEAR

The Black Bear of the Mountains are much the same species of those in the States. In comparison with the Grizzly it is entirely harmless. It is seldom found in the plains but inhabits the Timbered and mountainous districts. They are not very numerous and their habits are too well known to need a detailed description here.

Contemporary Stories from Around the State

The Funniest, Sorriest, or Most Bizarre Stories That I Heard

As I was traversing Colorado to write this book, I popped into every CPW or state park office I passed and asked, "Got any good bear stories?" Invariably, someone did—most often, *everyone* in the office did. Word spread, and pretty soon I was getting emails and calls from strangers and friends alike. In addition, I went through recent newspaper accounts and accumulated my favorite tidbits here and there.

I don't pretend to have heard all the stories from around the state, but I heard a great many. What follows are my favorite contemporary stories:

Hey Bear, Hey Bear, Hey Bear!

CRESTED BUTTE—Andy and Gail Sovick had just moved into their sixth house in six years in Crested Butte. "We're seasoned enough to mountain towns to know how to coexist with bears," Andy Sovick told me. "We've lived in their territory in Durango, Idaho, and Alaska. We're good with our trash and outdoor food. But apparently the local bears have been doing homework and brain exercises to adapt to man's inventions."

The third night in their new house, Sovick began his tale, he was just in that state between reality and dreaming when Gail stirred and said "Did you hear that?"

She does this often, so I mumbled and stubbornly continued on my path to REM. An indefinite amount of time later, Gail woke me again and said, 'I think there's something in the house.' I allowed reality to slide back into view and listened intently, hear nothing and put my head down. No more than point-oh-three seconds after I put my head down, a stool in the kitchen crashed across the floor and into a cabinet. *Dangit,* I thought, as I assumed my husbandly duty of putting on my pants and going off to face whatever danger had entered my home. *This is why men buy guns to defend their homes,* I thought, *and they despise this bare-handed and half-naked male role that was nowhere in the script of the wedding ceremony and vows.* The only gun in my house is a flint lock muzzle loader rifle for hunting elk, and would take me about three minutes to load. I could grab it, but only for use as a club. In this particular case, I went forward bare-handed running a list of scenarios through my fuzzy head—maybe it was a marmot or fox, or most likely, a drunk person wandering into the wrong home."

And that's when his list of possibilities ended. He continued, "Had I thought longer, I may have thought up a wiser move than what I ultimately chose. My typical strategy for dealing with unknown, potentially dangerous things in the night has always worked thus far. I've developed this strategy while camping, hiking, living among so many creatures (or drunks) who are interested in my food or heat. The strategy is as follows: Assess how close and where the critter is (or how drunk it is). Make a sudden and violent movement such as jumping up, clapping or opening a door aggressively. Then yell with the most macho voice I can muster one of the following phrases: *Who the heck is it!!??* or *Get Outta Here!!!* or in my less creative moments: *Hey!* On this particular night, I chose the first listed phrase while opening the bedroom door quickly and jumping into the hallway with my hands in a sort of wrestler pose. The enormous dark bear-like figure lumbering down the hall no more than two feet from my skinny wrestler arms was unimpressed. As quickly as I had jumped out to perform my manly move (which started out as I-wear-the-pants-and-protect-my-home-manly, and finished as I-am-stupid-and-this-is-why-men-don't-carry-children-manly), I jumped right back in, slammed the door behind me, stood up straight, gathered myself, and said calmly and matter-of-factly to Gail: "There's a bear in the house."

Gail: "A bear?!"
Andy: "A bear."
Gail: "What do we do?"
Andy: "Run."

Fortunately, there was a sliding door from the bedroom to the outdoor patio to which we rushed. We ran outside into the September air. This was probably smart. What was not so smart was what we did next (and please keep in mind, I had been half-dreaming just thirty seconds ago and was not quite on my A-game). Gail said "What if it comes into the bedroom?" The logical thing to do would be to say, "So what, let's get the hell out of here and call the marshal." What I did instead was run inside, Gail following, and proceeded to move a dresser awkwardly in front of the door. I'm still not sure why I did that.

At this point, I thought I could open the garage door, find a long club-like implement and try to encourage the bear to leave the way it came in. I ran around to the garage door. It was dark but I could see well enough to notice that the garage door was in fact open half-way. Brain moving a bit quicker now, it occurred to me the bear had lifted the door open and got in that way. As soon as I realized this, the huge furry intruder ran out of the opening below the door into the driveway and once again, only two feet from my skinny self. I turned to run again, only to run directly into Gail. This would have been a fantastic opportunity for *Ursus americanus* to grab us both and make a well supplied hibernation menu. Instead, it ran down the driveway and we ran into the garage and shut the door behind us. After ensuring the bear could not enter the house any way short of jumping through a window (let's hope they don't reach that point), we went back to our bedroom. But wait...we'd put the dresser in front of the bedroom door! I ventured back outside, clapping and yelling "Hey bear, hey bear, hey bear" (also an old practiced strategy) and re-entered the bedroom from the patio and let Gail in.

CANNIBALISM, BEAR STYLE

BACA—Peter Anderson explained it to me this way: In 2002, there was a bad drought year, and bears became...cannibals. Peter Anderson's house was broken into by a bear, but then it got ugly. He told me: "We had a small window in our back door which was left slightly open. While we were away from home (thankfully), a bear tore the screen off, pried the window open, and made its way into our kitchen. We had a freezer full of venison, elk, and bear meat. The bear ate it all. So I guess they'll eat their own as long as the meat is frozen!"

THE BIGGEST LOSER

CRAIG—In 2011, Richard Kendall may have set a state record

by shooting a 703-pound black bear he killed. He also gets my "Biggest Loser Award." Why? Kendall crawled into the bear's cave and shot it while it was hibernating.

Although the kill was legal at the time, Kendall was cited for shining a flashlight in the bruin's eyes and fined $68. Using artificial light to aid in hunting is illegal in Colorado.

Since then, politicians put a new law on the books: hibernating black bears will no longer be fair game for Colorado hunters. The new law was proposed after the outcry that came in response to this bear, which many hunters have described as unsportsmanlike and unethical, because the animal was not in the open but was resting in a secure place. The regulation now states, "No person shall hunt, take or harass a bear in its den."

DON'T SHOOT YOUR FOOT OFF BEFORE YOU LOOK

BUFFALO PASS—On the fifth day of a seven-day solo wilderness trek, Eric Hermann had dropped down from timberline to camp near Lake Diana in northern Colorado, near the Wyoming border. A friend had talked him into carrying a .38 Special revolver to keep him "safe from bears and weirdos," and, as he told me, "for the fifth night in a row I had loaded five of the six magazine ports and placed the gun, hammer down on the unloaded port, next to my head."

He was sleeping fine when he was awakened by a loud roar—at least a sleeper's fuzzy memory of a loud roar—which could have been anything, from thunder to a supersonic jet to a bear's roar. He told the story like this:

> Drifting back to sleep, I became aware of something reaching into the tent and, well, sort of fondling my leg. My eyes were very wide now, and heart pounding, when I sprang up to a seat aiming the flashlight at the tent door.
>
> Nothing! Oh, well. I drifted back toward sleep only to feel the same brushing of my shin.

Some bear must be reaching in to test my tenderness, I thought, then sprang up again—this time with headlamp *and* pistol, cocking it as I swept it forward.

I was aiming point-blank at a terrified deer mouse balanced on my shin, his eyes so huge, and I swear he raised both his little front legs in surrender—hands up!

Attempting then to retreat, his legs began to run frantically along my sleeping bag, but it was too slippery, so they just scurried nowhere, as if he were on ice.

Being a lousy pistol shot, and being shocked from this attack, I probably would have missed the mouse and... well, even if I'd hit him, I would have taken out my right foot.

The next day I decided I'd better fire the damn gun, so I did, and the report shook the entire forest around me. I had heard nothing but wind, birds, water, and coyotes for five days, and this seemed explosive. I yelled an apology to the forest and put the silly gun away.

I bet that mouse got to Wyoming before I did.

Veterinarians and U-Hauls

FORT COLLINS—Dr. Terry Campbell sees all sorts of animals at Colorado State University's Veterinarian Teaching Hospital. It's no surprise that he sees bears, too, whether they're black bears from a circus or grizzlies from the zoo. Sometimes they're delivered in fancy trailers, sometimes they're brought in with U-Hauls—but in all cases, post-op care is a bit of a trick. Such is the life of a vet.

One of Terry's favorite bears, he told me, was Bart the Bear, the famous male Alaskan Kodiak bear that starred in movies such as Legends of the Fall, Clan of the Cave Bear, and Into the Wild. In 1998, Bart made an appearance at the 70th Academy Awards as part of a salute to animal actors. John Candy, Dan Aykroyd, Gregory Peck, Brad Pitt, Alec

Baldwin, and Anthony Hopkins all appeared in films opposite the bear—and apparently were happy with his training, which was good, since he weighted 1800 pounds.

But not all was well, and Bart was limping. His trainer brought him to CSU's vet hospital, and the vets there gave the bear a spoon covered in honey mixed with opiate. "The bear licked it right up," Terry told me. "Once he was asleep, we wheeled him into radiology and took some images. Unfortunately, there was a tumor, eating away at the bone."

Since bears put about 60 percent of their weight on their hind legs, Terry recommended amputating the forelimb—but the trainer, he said, "just couldn't do it." The bear was taken home, and Bart was eventually euthanized. According to his unofficial website, Bart died peacefully surrounded by his family and friends at his home on May 10, 2000.

I Don't Have Bear Insurance

Chuck's Cabin, Vail Pass—Three huts are huddled in the wilderness near Vail Pass, accessible only by cross-country skis or snowshoes in the winter. Once I'm past the buzzing of the snowmobiles and the traffic of I-70, and have skied into the silence of the Holy Cross Wilderness and the Sawatch Range, I feel the remote peacefulness of the place. I'm at 11,200 feet, heading toward Shrine Pass, where I'll have a view of Mount of the Holy Cross—the northernmost 14er (as Coloradoans call their mountain peaks of 14,000 feet or higher) in the state, named for the distinctive cross-shaped snowfield on the northeast face.

The three huts are owned by the 10th Mountain Division Hut Association—named in honor of the soldiers of the 10th Mountain Division of the U.S. Army, who trained during World War II at Camp Hale nearby. Based in Aspen, the nonprofit manages a system of 29 backcountry huts throughout the state, which are connected by over 350 miles of trails. As

I listen to the swish of my skis and the soft sound of planting my poles, I consider that this area is about as silent as one can get in the Colorado Rockies.

But this area was not always so quiet. There used to be a high-end restaurant up here, and Mark Schoenecker, along with his former wife, the chef, used to run it. "Chuck's Cabin used to be a restaurant, open from June to the end of September," he told me. The possibility of a restaurant smack dab in the middle of the White River National Forest blows my mind—and in fact, the reason this eighty acres is private land is a bit of a mystery. The parcel was neither a homestead nor a mining claim, but was purchased for cash by the Roosevelt Administration in 1904. Legend has it that Roosevelt may have wanted to make it his own personal hunting camp. Some have also speculated that the land was to be used as a destination for pilgrims coming to view the Mount of the Holy Cross, or perhaps was tied in some way with the old mine site just northwest of the property. In any case, the possibility of a restaurant in wilderness is an oddity—I'm guessing it's the only one in the state.

Surrounded by such wilderness, it's not surprising that the restaurant and bears would eventually meet up.

"Back behind Chuck's Cabin is a meadow," Mark said, as he began his story:

> I built a platform up there on the hill, with a ten-by-ten tent, and a gorgeous view. I was tired of commuting from Vail every day. So I slept there, with a queen-sized futon, a lamp—pretty cushy considering the setting. And in the front area of Chuck's Cabin there was a big stove, which was used by the baker/pastry chef, and Regina would cook a big pot of bones for *jus* or soup stock overnight.
>
> It was toward the end of the summer, and things were starting to wind down. It was the first week in September, I was sleeping, and at about five in the morning, I

woke up and I heard a bear. He was coming toward the tent. My first thought was, *Oh no, what did I bring in here? Did I break one of my cardinal rules and bring in food?* I hadn't. But the bear was still coming. I heard him snorting and shuffling around, right outside the tent. He stepped on the platform, and the whole thing moved. He then put his paw on the fabric and began pressing in. I lifted my head, and his paw lands right where my head was, on the pillow. His face is just a foot and a half away from mine; I could see it through the tent. He was so close I could smell him. I was a bit panicked, couldn't think of what to do, so I screamed *"Boo!"* at the top of my lungs. Next thing I knew, I heard him give a shocked grunt, and he ran off noisily into the woods. Without hesitation, I grabbed my sleeping bag and pillow and high-tailed it down to my truck, which had a topper, and I went back to sleep.

I was woken up a little later by the pastry chef, who had just shown up. He says to me, "We had a bear last night," and I say, "No kidding." At this point, there was light, so we surveyed the damage. We had an area with about six hundred-quart coolers out there with white wine, sodas, drinks. The bear had tossed all that, drunk a few Cokes. Bit right through the cans and sucked the liquid out. I bet by the time he got to me, he was pretty amped up. The carnage was wide and complete. The forty-quart stock pot was pulled off the stove, and the bear had dragged it half way to Jay's cabin, about fifty yards. After that, I got a shotgun and dog, but I kept staying in the tent.

One year later, Mark said he had upgraded to a hard-sided camper. And then this happened:

> I had a couple of containers outside, plastic ones, with no food or anything, but just stuff. Same deal: I'm sleep-

ing, and at about five-thirty in morning, right before light, I heard a bear rooting around out there. I started yelling, but he wasn't scared—he was still moving containers. I was too afraid to hop out of the trailer, so I sat in there patiently waiting. I knew the current pastry chef was going to get there soon—she always got there at quarter to six. I didn't hear the bear, but I did hear the car on the gravel. So just as she's about to pull up, I run out to her car, and get inside. As we pull up to park at the restaurant, a beautiful cinnamon-colored black bear ambles away in the headlights of the car—pretty small—maybe a year or two old.

Later that same day, we served lunch, as usual. We served several hundred lunches each day. We shut down at two-thirty, and the night staff arrived at four for dinner set-up. This was fine dining at night, reservation only, we sold out every single night. So we had the staff polishing the glasses, setting tables, getting linens out. One of the waitresses had a dog who started barking. "My dog never barks," she said, "there's something going on."

She walks back toward her car, parked by the dumpster and the generator shed—this is right before the first guests arrive—and then she's flying back to the restaurant, yelling "There's a bear in the dumpster!"

I go storming out to the camper, grab a shotgun, get loaded up, and start walking back. A bear pops his head out of dumpster. I yell "Get out of here!" and he goes cruising into the woods. My first guests had already shown up, and a bear is right behind the restaurant! I grab my shotgun and begin creeping around the side of the restaurant, toward the back of the cabin. Behind me is the sous chef, armed with a chef's knife, and behind him are a couple of wait staff, and a few kitchen help. It's like a cartoon. I peer around the corner, and the bear looks at me. I let a couple of rounds go into the air. The bear bolts. I'm faced at this point with guests who've just heard a couple of gun shots. So I stroll into the dining room, with the shotgun resting on my shoulder, and tell them I've just scared off a bear. They look amused, and let me know that I should have included them in the episode. All I could think to say was: "I don't have any bear liability insurance."

Castro, Bathrooms, Bears

ALAMOSA—Aaron Abeyta's pickup truck was covered in dust as we leaned against it and stared at the late-summer faded landscape of the San Juan Mountains to the west, the Sangre de Cristos to the east. We were standing on ground near Alamosa that has been in his family for seven generations, which is about six generations longer than most can claim, and close to being as many as is possible, in recorded history, at least. His family came to far-southern Colorado in the 1840s to ranch, run sheep, grow hay, and make lives along the Conejos River. One hundred-seventy years later, we stood near windswept adobe buildings, champe (wild roses) from which his family has always made jelly, and a family cemetery with graves dating back to the original landowners, long before Colorado was a state.

His family still ranches land near where his great-great grandfather first settled, and our conversation eventually turned to bears—which are plentiful in this area—and I asked him how many sheep his family loses. "Ah, just one or two a year," he said. "Now we have dogs. Dogs are way worse than bears in terms of losses. They pack up and just maim... they don't even kill the animals."

If anyone has good stories, it's the Abeyta family, and so I asked him to tell me one about bears.

"Cubano" means Cuban, Aaron explained, and that's what

the family's sheepherder from Cuba has been called since his arrival in this country. For twenty-seven years, Cubano has been a sheepherder for the Abeyta family—following the sheep from mountain pasture to mountain pasture, camping in the solitary life, living in a trailer or a tent.

The history of how Cubano got here is not as peaceful: At the age of six or seven, he was caught stealing bananas. He was arrested by Cuban authorities and thrown into prison. He spent his childhood there, not receiving even the most rudimentary education—to this day, he cannot spell or decipher numbers. At one point, his ankles were broken, and he now walks on the inside edges of his feet, his ankles clearly turned at odd angles. It was during the Mariel boatlift of 1980 that Cubano escaped to the States—part of an exodus organized by Cuban-Americans with the agreement of Cuban president Fidel Castro (later, it was discovered that a number of the exiles had been released from jails; Castro publicly stated "I have flushed the toilets of Cuba on the United States.")

How Cubano got to Colorado is a bit of a mystery, Aaron admitted, but he knows that Cubano has been no criminal. On the contrary, he has been a quiet and honorable man making a living. "He's been an upstanding dude with little to no exposure to the world," Aaron told me. For a long time, in fact, Cubano tried to seek out his mother back in Cuba; eventually, he did, and she was able to send him a photo.

"Cubano is a real character," Aaron said. "In the twenty-plus years he's worked for us, he's never asked us for soap or a brush. I only mention that because the only time he took a very long bath—several in succession, actually—was for my grandfather's funeral. I think he thought of my grandpa as his father figure. The only time any of us can remember him a little sick was the time he was attempting to quick draw and shot himself in the foot. He made it to the hospital for that one."

That, and one other time that almost cost him his life. "We think now that Cubano was new to bacon. Or bacon was new to him," Aaron said. "I was about 13 at the time, helping my parents on the ranch. We took him a box of raw bacon on a Saturday—we always brought him groceries at his camp, which was deep in the Cruces Basin Wilderness area. When we came back the next Saturday, we came over a ridge and saw ten sheep, then five more, then ten—we knew something was wrong right away. Sheep don't normally scatter like that."

Aaron and his family found Cubano curled up in his tent, deathly ill. He had eaten the bacon raw, apparently.

Aaron's brother went for medicine, and Aaron attended to Cubano and then went to get the sheep. "I went into this dark clearing, surrounded by spruce, and man, it stunk. In the corner was a pile of sheep five or six feet high, ten feet wide," Aaron recalled. "I figured out what had happened. A bear had piled them up and covered them in pine needles."

Startled at the sight and smell, Aaron debated what to do. He knew that when a sheep dies, you cut off its tail or ear. "So, I figure I better do that, so I could count how many died. So there I am, counting, when suddenly I hear breaking branches. I don't stick around. I took off running. Like, Carl Lewis speed."

In the end, all ended well. The sheep were rounded up and Cubano got antibiotics—proving he could survive not only Castro's regime, but raw bacon and bears. Twelve sheep died, and the bear wandered off somewhere up the mountain.

No Time for Essentials

BORDER OF NEW MEXICO AND COLORADO—In 1983, Roger Arellano, a sheepherder, was camped near a stand of aspen trees, on a little knoll near the border of Colorado and New Mexico.

It was one of the last camps of the year, in the autumn—right as bears are getting ready for hibernation. When visitors went up to bring him food, they saw flies everywhere. The reason, they soon discovered, was a dead bear.

How'd the bear end up that way? Arellano had a habit of never getting of his horse without his gun—a habit he developed after a horse had run off with his rifle in his scabbard and broke it to pieces. He had a 30-30 Winchester lever action, and every time he got off the horse, the rifle went with him. He never, *ever* got off a horse without his rifle.

This time was no exception: This particular day, a bear had killed a couple of sheep. Roger was on the lookout for them, but he had to answer nature's call. Right in the middle of his business, the horse bolted. Roger turned around—and there was a bear, charging him. Roger's pants and shorts were around his ankles, his chaps too—all caught in his cowboy boots and spurs. Although bears do false charges all the time, he didn't want to take his chances, and he shot.

"The bear was within five feet," the rancher told me. "I'm pretty sure he didn't have time to wipe."

THE CASE OF THE DIAMOND NECKLACE

SAN ISABEL NATIONAL FOREST—Rose Bayless was working in the Colorado State Forest office in Salida when her diamond necklace, a present from her husband, broke and fell off her neck. She took it off, put it in a bag, and put the bag in her lunch box, so that she wouldn't lose it. When she got home, in a neighborhood bordering the San Isabel National Forest, she accidentally threw her lunch in the trash, and her husband actually took the trash out ("It was an amazing day," she joked to me). She remembered the necklace in the middle of the night, and promised herself to get it out first thing. But in the morning, her husband had news for her: "Honey, there's a bear in the dumpster!" The bear, in fact, was *stuck* in the dumpster—he had pried the lid open, but it had fallen back in on him. She called CPW, but by the time they arrived, the bear had managed to open the door and get out. The entire dumpster was trashed—there was no hope in finding her necklace—but all's well that ends well—her husband bought her a new one.

Velvet's Lesson

BRECKENRIDGE—What do mama bears do when their cubs are in danger? Send them up high.

That simple behavioral trait usually serves them well. But not too many years ago it was the birth of a tragedy in Summit County.

In the Blue Lakes region, some out-of-towner house sitters had done the typical: put their trash out the night before pickup. Unsurprisingly, a mother with two cubs came prowling—bears are smart opportunists, after all. When a dog shot out of the house to bark at the bears, the mother bear sent her cubs to scramble up the nearest thing around—a telephone pole. Once they got up to safety, the sow went up too, hit the transceiver, and was electrocuted. The cubs, however, survived.

Orphaned and only five months old, the cubs remained at the top of the pole, bawling for their mother. The community sprung into action quickly: The mother was removed, and Xcel Energy came with a cherry-picker for the cubs. "We got them off and transported the cubs to the best wildlife rehab facility in the area, which is in Silt," Gail Marshall told me. She's the creator of Summit County Bear Aware and locally known as the go-to person for all things bear.

Several months later, in the winter, Marshall got a call from the rehab facility. "The cubs were old enough to be released. Did I want to go? Yes I did. They were called Cubs 78 and 79, although I called them Audrey and Maureen [for

Hepburn and O'Hara]." She added that she wasn't allowed to talk about their release for some time—part of policy is to keep mum about relocations to ensure the animals' safety. "But I can tell you now," she said. "We released them up near Heaney. I've gotten several reports that they were seen fishing, denning, being natural bears. They lived and have had cubs themselves. They're all doing fine. It's a story that turned out okay."

While there are some success stories, and while Summit County Bear Smart, CPW, and the wildlife foundation will do their part, there continue to be surprising lapses is common sense. Last summer, for example, a sow and two cubs had to be destroyed in the Breckenridge area. A neighborhood had taken to feeding a bear at the base of Peak 8, and when Marshall went to give one of her talks, she found out that one of the renters asked a homeowner to keep putting out food for the bears—they'd been feeding bears for months. "I was flabbergasted when I heard that," Marshall noted. "First, that is *so* illegal; second, it's dangerous for the renters; and third; you're putting wildlife in danger."

That incident brought to light a bigger story: The whole neighborhood named the bear, and "Velvet" had lost her fear of humans, a trait she passed on to her cubs. The homeowners association even was sending out announcements about Velvet's visits.

"We had to trap the mother and two cubs, and there was nothing we could do to rehab her or relocate her," Marshall said. "The situation was too far advanced. She had to be put down. It really broke a lot of people's hearts. They were saying, 'Oh, how cute, how cute, the bear,' but it's *not* cute. You're not saving a bear by feeding it. It was pretty upsetting. Their deaths simply could have been avoided," Marshall said.

That's the sort of thing she wants people to know about, although Marshall noted that the situation has vastly improved vastly in Breckenridge and the surrounding area in the last few years. "Years ago, we had a trash ordinance and it wasn't being enforced. But things are different now," Marshall said. "Community service officers do hand out citations and that makes a big difference. There's a wildlife management program in the works, and county commissioners are working on one for the unincorporated areas. Our town council is also very supportive of protecting our bears. Things are looking good."

And how long is she going to keep doing this? When I asked her, she paused. "Well, I'll keep doing it until it doesn't need to be done."

Bear vs. Germ

A Personal Look at the Danger Factor

Like many Coloradoans, I feel safer camping than I do in a city—although there's always the chance of danger, especially when it comes to other *people* in the mountains. That's what I was thinking as I watched a couple meander over to my family's remote campsite. My brain registered the .45s holstered on their belts, along with serious knives and cans of pepper spray.

"Thought you could use some wood," the woman said, plopping down her load near our fire. Her husband followed suit. My two children, surprised by the visitors, stopped eating their Spaghettios, which were dripping down their faces, and I glanced at my husband, indicating the couple's guns with my eyes.

We were car camping (not our preferred method, but we were traveling a long distance), with no other campers around anywhere except for this highly weaponed couple. As usual, my family was prepared in a half-assed way, the result of having young children, jobs, and a foolhardy belief in Jane Austen's famous quote, "How often is happiness destroyed by preparation, foolish preparation!"

"That's very nice of you," I said, indicating the wood.

"Thanks." I did not state the obvious, which was that there was plenty of firewood around, and their offering was simply an excuse to come over to check us out as worthy tent-neighbors for the night.

"There are lots of bears," the woman said, after introducing herself.

"Okay," I said. "We know about that."

She looked doubtful but nodded. "Just wanted to warn you."

"We know all about it," I said again, smiling.

After they left, my kids looked up at us. "We're safe, right? You said we're safe."

"Bears," I said, "are not what we need to worry about."

An hour earlier, my son had sliced his thumb on his new pocketknife. Not a deep slice, but a wide wedge of skin was flapping around. Nothing too major, and he didn't make a sound. But unexpected and rare tears sprang to my eyes at the exact moment the blood sprang from the depth of his body—not because the cut was serious, but because of what was spreading across my own back.

A few weeks before, I had undergone surgery. Right before our departure, a bunch of "bug bites" appeared on my back, which I soon realized weren't bites. I had the very thing I didn't want—a staph infection, one that had gone systemic and was starting to look bad. We were set to leave on this camping road-trip, and I had just enough time to force myself ("Oh, yes, you *will* fit me in today") into my doctor's schedule to get an antibiotic.

As we gathered around the fire, I watched my son re-bandage his dirty hand, and I was surprised by a sudden and enormous flush—the simple yet terrible fear of death. Oh, how fragile my family was, in the flickering light. And oh, how little control we have, although we like to pretend otherwise with our germ-killers and sterile bandages and guns and pepper spray.

The fact is: Life is a terminal disease. And we all have it. And that simple truth can make us crazy with pain and fear. And we tend, I think, to turn that fear toward large animals, such as bears, rather than the things that will really get us.

OF COURSE, any animal that can grow to be up to 200 or 400 pounds (or even more, occasionally) has the potential to be dangerous, and is easily capable of harming a human if it wants to, but the fact remains that black bears are, for the most part, docile and timid. I am millions of times more likely to be killed by a car, by lightning, by a dog, or by another human. Even when in the middle of bear country, as I was then, my chances of being murdered are (according to one statistical site) about 40,000 times greater.

The 750,000 black bears of North America kill less than one person per year, on the average. Worldwide, grizzlies kill about five people a year. In Colorado, there have been only three deaths from black bears since records have been kept.

Which is to say: One of the safest places a person can be is in the woods.

THE ONLY THING to do with fear is turn it into an adventure, and let fear guide us and show us the way. That's why, at times like this, that I like to think of Peter Pan's dictum to Wendy: "Well, you know, life is a *very* grand adventure!"

So that's what I said to my children as we continued our journey the next day. They thought I was talking about bears, but that is not what I meant. What I did not say was this: On average, one or two people die per year in this country due to a bear attack, and about 30 are injured. On the other hand, last year, 95,000 Americans got serious and invasive MRSA infections (the drug-resistant kind of staph infection that has been on the rise in recent decades) and more than 18,000 of them died. Most of them—85 percent of the infected, and 92 percent of those who died—got MRSA in health care settings.

It's true that folks in my age group fare pretty well in fighting staph. Still, after a few days, it became clear that the antibiotic I was on wasn't working at all. I had open and infectious wounds, my son's cut was still deep and puffy (and the kids were re-injuring themselves on a daily basis), I had a parent's deep obligation to keep myself and my children safe, and I was starting to feel that sick-uncomfortable feeling in my stomach.

Historically, I have not been much of a worrier—I am unprepared and undisturbed and too busy. Every once in a while, though, I have to work hard at getting rid of *fear*, since fear is the main thing that makes suffering possible ("Nothing is so much to be feared as fear itself," said Henry David Thoreau, who probably paraphrased Francis Bacon: "Nothing is terrible except fear itself." This is the sort of thing I have tacked up in my office. I think it's supposed to help calm me in times of need, but all it does is confirm that lots of smart people in the world have understood that fear is the worst disease to have.)

"Life is a very grand adventure," I sing-songed as we hiked and camped, but I was acutely aware of the invisible enemy among us, and that we walk a razor's edge.

THE BOOK *Infection: The Uninvited Universe,* written by Coloradoan Gerald Callahan, is one of my favorites. He's a microbiologist-pathologist who's interested in the bacteria, parasites, fungi, and viruses in our body—and how they make us who we are. Because he's an acquaintance of mine, I emailed him during this trip (when I was able to get Internet access) about my dilemma, hoping for some comfort about how strong immune systems are. "Bacteria, like bears," he emailed me back, "mostly keep to themselves, and the vast majority of bacteria inside of human beings are helpful. The problem arises out of simple mathematics. Let's say one percent of bears are potential people-killers (and that's probably a significant overestimate) and just .001 percent of bacteria are potential people killers. Let's just say there's about 200,000 brown/grizzly bears in the world—that's 2,000 killer bears spread over hundreds of thousands of square miles. On the other hand, there are about 10^{29} bacteria in the world. One percent of 10^{29} is 10^{24}. That is about 100,000,000,000,000 bacteria for every man, woman, and child on this planet!"

Which just confirmed my suspicion: Encounters with bears, especially killer bears, are extremely rare. Encounters with bacteria are our way of life, and even though only a very tiny fraction of those bacteria have anything other than our best interests at heart, sicknesses and deaths are a mathematical certainty.

I just didn't want to be one of the stricken, not yet.

I PICKED UP the second antibiotic at a very tiny medical office. The next day, I had an allergic reaction to it, and the staph infection was deeper and redder. "Life is a very grand adventure!" I said to my kids as we drove through the mountains to visit the clinic again. At this point, I realized my mantra was a whistling-in-the-dark sort of thing; through gritted teeth and seething with fear. My kids, luckily, did not seem to notice.

When she saw me, the doctor stood back and scratched her ear. "Yeah, probably MRSA," she said, looking about as unhappy as I felt. "But don't worry too much. One more try, and then we'll get you to the hospital." We both knew that if this third antibiotic didn't do the trick, I could always get intravenous antibiotic. Surely, something could be done for me there. Right?

Stomach-achy (from the antibiotics) and yeast infected (also from the antibiotics), I started on this newest drug, kept quiet about my hidden fears, and kept an eye on my son's thumb, and both my children's bodies. We kept hiking, paddled across a lake, camped.

"How are you feeling?" my husband would ask occasionally.

"Life is a very grand adventure," I'd answer.

Each night, in the tent, my husband would lift up my shirt and examine my back. One evening, he said, "Hey, no joke, Laura, it's better!"

"Really?"

"Really."

I went outside and examined my son's hand: healed up, no signs of infection. I breathed a sincere sigh of great relief, and I must admit, a few tears flew into my eyes. No big grizzly, no gun-wielding camper, and no microscopic germ was going to get me. Not yet, at least.

Then I went to sit by the fire. None of us was going to die. Not yet. But if we had, via bear or germ, I hoped I'd go with a sense of adventure and bravery in my heart. Because while being afraid of death is a no-brainer regular thing, I'd like to face it down with a smile and a wink. Not because death is not serious—it *is*—but because I want to face fear with a smile that acknowledges the mystery of it all.

WINNER, HANDS DOWN

A TRIBUTE TO
THE MUTANTS,
BOTH OLD AND NEW

IT'S A QUESTION worth considering: Who, in the end, spends the most time with Colorado's bears? Who gets to know them best, both as a species and as the individuals they are?

The answer, I believe, lies not with a hunter, camper, logger, photographer, or outdoors-person—but rather with Uncle Sam. Or, rather, certain federal- or state-employed individuals who, by far, outrank us all when it comes to hours spent with wild bears. Hundreds of bears, hundreds of hours, hundreds of stories that involve blizzards, dens, bluff-charging bears, exhaustion, and cuddling cubs.

These are Colorado's Mutants.

TO CLARIFY: the renowned Colorado black bear biologist, Tom Beck, began dubbing his group of researchers and field workers "The Mutants" back in the 1980s. By this, he meant the group of folks who'd been trekking through the mountains finding and studying bears—conducting what was the first bear research in the state. One of them was John Broderick, who, when I asked him to clarify what "The Mutants" meant, told me, "Oh, you know. The people who are weird enough to want to walk around with a roadkill carcass in their hands. Or those who cross-country ski for ten miles in a blizzard and build a snow cave so that they can collar a bear the next day. Cold, wet, smelly, exhausted, crazy people..."

"Yeah," researcher Dave Lewis chimed in—he's from the new generation of bear-researchers, more or less protégés of the early Mutants. "Those of us who like it when the maggots push the lid off a fifty-five-gallon drum of rotting stuff! That's when you're a mutant."

He looked at me and smiled, obviously quietly proud to be part of such a group.

So, who specifically are Colorado's mutants? There are the old school, wizened leaders, one of them being John Broderick, a district wildlife manager and then the State Terrestrial Biologist. He started working for Tom Beck in the early 1980s, conducting the first black bear captures in Colorado. Now a senior wildlife biologist for the state, he has handled literally hundreds of bears. There's also the new young generation of bear-loving researchers, two of whom are Sharon Baruch-Mordo and David Lewis, both finishing advanced degrees that focus on bear-human conflicts. Then there are the in-betweeners, people like Lisa Wolfe, Colorado's State Wildlife Field Veterinarian, and Stewart Breck, a carnivore ecologist and researcher for the USDA National Wildlife Research Center.

These people often find themselves working together (in various configurations) in the Colorado mountains, snowshoeing up a hill or climbing into bear dens, brought together by their curiosity and serious study of bears.

I figured that there's nothing like snow-camping at 10,000 feet and hanging with a teeth-popping, aggravated bear to draw you together, and to get to know bears—and so I brought them together to ask about their favorite bears, their favorite moments, and their fears and hopes for the bruins of Colorado.

DESPITE THE high number of advanced degrees that were around me, I saw no signs of shirt, tie, or smooth hands. Dr. Lisa Wolfe, for example, has published papers on such topics as "PrP in Rectal Lymphoid Tissue of Deer" and "Oral Papillomatosis in Canada Lynx," but the only Google images you'll find of her are photos from out in the field, red-nosed from the cold and smiling, holding bear cubs. Although she's a small and attractive woman, she carries herself like someone who can face a bear without flinching—which she regularly does. As the state field veterinarian, she spends a lot of time with wild animals doing what she called "assisting with field capture and sampling," which in my language means that if she's not out culturing big horn sheep, she's giving a shot to a mountain lion or darting a bear in a bear den.

Ditto Stewart Breck, whose online bio says something about his working on nonlethal methods for preventing conflict, and population biology and behavioral ecology of carnivores. His academic papers sound properly intellectual ("Using Genetic Relatedness to Investigate the Development of Conflict Behavior in Black Bears"), but there was no sign of an ivory tower here. He showed up to our gathering looking like he was going camping, as did John Broderick, Sharon Baruch-Mordo, and Dave Lewis. They're all highly respected in their fields, and their research is intellectually fascinating—but the love of outdoors was in their eyes, and their calm, steady personalities illustrated the ability to accept things like maggots and bear scat and blood and guts. And when I surreptitiously glanced around at their hands, I saw evidence of people who know how to lug a bear from her den, how to draw blood samples, or how to hold up an avalanche shovel for protection in case a bluff-charge isn't as bluff as they are hoping for. No one could accuse these people of being soft academics; they look tougher than loggers or hunters, and if I were a bear, I wouldn't mess with them.

When I asked them why they picked bears, I got a lot of blank stares, as if I were asking something so obvious that they were worried about my mental health. But it was a legitimate question—surely they felt something powerful for bears specifically, or they wouldn't put up with the required Mutant part of their behavior—after all, not everyone wants to go crawling in bear dens in wet, cold, and dangerous conditions—and I wanted them to put words to it.

Steward Breck tilted his head, considering. "Well," he said, "I will say that of all the species I've worked with, the bears are the most fascinating. And frankly, they just have a high cuteness factor. I try to be objective. I don't want to anthropomorphize. But you can't help it."

Lisa Wolfe agreed. "We try to be scientific and objective. But the fact is, we get to know these bears as individuals. You know, we do what's called 'backtracking'—we download information from the GPS collar on the bear and then follow the locations to see what the bear was doing that day or 'what resources they were using.' We see what rock they turned over for ants, see where they went through the day. Those little details—you just get to know the bears. If people knew as much as about these individuals as we do, for example, they'd just put their trash away."

Sharon Baruch-Mordo shrugged, as if that explained it all, and then added, "Those moments of handling the bear are the best rewards—one of the happiest moments in my life was the first time I held a cub."

"Their speed and agility," Dave Lewis threw in.

"They're intelligent, imagistic," someone else said.

"They're big, furry, charismatic..."

"Smart, savvy, adaptable..."

"They're powerful, but not vicious," someone else added.

"Oh, and take hibernation, for instance," Wolfe said. "Isn't that fascinating? A fascinating adaptive technique? Physiologically, they can do this thing we can't do, go into this deep sleep."

"And how they've adapted to humans, too," Breck stated. "For example, they know to go up to mini vans more than to other cars, since there tends to be more food in mini vans."

Several noted that one particularly endearing quality about bears is the strong maternal instinct: "A mother bear will always gather her cubs up in her arms when I come in," Wolfe said. "She'll rock and rock them. She may pop her lips and 'talk' to you, but she's not going to get up and leave her cubs. There's this idea that mother bears are vicious and threatening. But I tell you, they are not going to leave those babies."

Dave Lewis, the youngest of the team, threw in, "I thought I knew some stuff about black bears when I started working on the project, but looking back I knew almost nothing and what I did know was incorrect. In general, humans still have a good deal to learn about bears."

John Broderick nodded. "Once you've worked with a bear, something makes you want to stick with it. They are so majestic. They evoke a certain amount of charm, they make you feel a certain level of integrity. You have a high fear, the work is physically dangerous, and it's the best work I've ever done." He shrugged, agreeing with himself. "The work doesn't come easy, but the reward therefore is great. That's empowering. Also, there's the fact that when you see them, you're dealing with an ancient response—to run—but you have to stop that. That's an interesting phenomenon. Also, they're so human. Native Americans considered them a brother to humans, and for good reason. They're a lot like us. They're large, are forward looking, they have good ears, and if you skinned one, you'd see that the musculature looked very human." He paused. "Yeah, I just don't feel the same way about ungulates."

THIS GROUP has dealt with many, many bears. Dave Lewis, for instance, although the newest member, has already handled about 90 individual bears, some of them multiple times. The project and study itself tracks about 125 individual bears, from cubs to what he calls "senior citizen bears." Of these, he has about 25 individuals that he knows well—he knows where they've hung out, their ages, den locations, and various other little stories that accumulate while the bears are being collared.

That's a lot of bears. Most people in Colorado are happy to see one or two in the wild. But these people have possibly touched as many (or more) bears than they have people—and that strikes me as simply wonderful.

The vast majority of the time, there are no real stories that come from their work. As in, the researcher's fieldwork work goes smoothly and follows a fairly predictable routine: The bear is tranquilized; a collar might be put on or removed, depending on the situation; blood is drawn; the bear is carefully put back; the bear wakes up and goes back to bear life.

That's the way it should be, and that's the way they like it. It's boring and there *are* no stories—that's the best possible scenario.

From time to time, however, things go a bit wrong—which maybe isn't what they want, but it's what makes a good story, and that's what I ask about.

One of the best stories, they agree, had to do with bears and the development of BAM, a cocktail of drugs used for tranquilizing. Lisa Wolfe and Sharon Baruch-Mordo had investigated this new tranquilizer combination for use in bears. There was a great advantage to BAM in that, unlike with other tranquilizers, bears could recover quickly from it—important, for example, in the summer or in urban environments, when it behooves the bear to be able to get up and move around quickly and without being drowsy. "It was really magical," Breck said. "A really great drug to use."

But once, it wasn't—and after all that, everything changed.

A group of scientists and CPW folks had gone out to check a sow with three yearlings in the Aspen area. They had her collared and were studying her for several years (for one of the studies about bear population and human-bear conflicts). The sow, they knew (from radio collar signals), had denned up deep in a very large mine shaft—about forty feet long. Unlike many bear dens, which are small and cramped, this one had ample room—enough for the entire group of people to fit in with the four sleeping bears. To get down into the mine, they lowered an old climbing rope (which they'd tied to a tree), which they used to help get up and down the steep slope.

"We tranquilized the four bears, who were in a nice nest," Breck said. "We were all working away, and Lisa, as always, was monitoring the bears and their respiration. She's always very careful about this. Then Lisa noticed one of the yearlings wasn't breathing well. Something was wrong, really wrong."

In order to ensure the safety of the yearling, they decided to reverse the drug. As the yearling was waking up, the other two yearlings started showing signs of distress, and so they were given a reversal drug as well. What followed next sounds, to me, like *barely*-controlled chaos: "That yearling just started hollering," Breck said. "We had one person sort of sitting on it, trying to keep it calm and quiet. Then there were two people on that yearling, and then there were about five. Man, that bear was *strong*."

It's wise to remember that yearlings, although young, are still around one hundred pounds. They were also persistent: the yearling did not, as hoped, calm down. In fact, the cub got more feisty, which started to cause a reaction in the still-drugged mother and the coming-out-of-druggedness siblings.

Rather quickly, the group decided to move the cubs out of the den, which necessitated a lot of pushing, pulling, heaving, and grunting—no injuries, Breck said, and then quickly added, "well, nothing serious" (and it occurred to me that these folks' definition of injury probably differs from mine).

One by one, the hundred-pound yearlings were hoisted up and out of the mine—and, once outside, they immediately calmed. "They got quiet, started milling about," Breck said. "It was a drastic change."

Meanwhile, Sharon Baruch-Mordo, the primary investigator, was still working with the sow, rapidly trying to finish the job at hand. She finished getting the new GPS collar programmed and fitted to the sow. Everyone left the sleeping sow except Wolfe and Wright, who stayed to monitor her after giving the reversal drug. In order to be sure it was working and the sow was fine, she prodded the bear. There was no response, so she poked the bear again. On the third poke, the bear woke. Kevin Wright, the district wildlife manager, who Wolfe described as "being the type that is always watching your back," said it was time to leave. "When he says it is time to leave, you don't question it," Wolfe explained. Wright quickly pulled himself up with the rope through the narrow entrance and reached down to pull her up. "He pulled me up with such force that I was airborne, and I landed on my feet." She chuckled. "That was a lot of force."

The adventure, however, was not over: they put the yearlings back into the mine shaft with the sow, and then started piling snow back in around the opening, as they always do. "There we were, pushing snow up, packing it in, and out shoots the sow's paw."

In a scene that makes me think of a horror movie—a claw darting out right at you—the sow had decided she was coming out. The researchers backed up, the bears came out. As it turned out, the bears came out rather casually, not aggressively, and the researchers gathered up their gear and backed into the trees. Their main goal was not to disturb the bears any more than they already had, and to make sure the yearlings and sow stayed together.

In the end, the humans moved away, and the bears moved to another den.

And that was the last time BAM was used on hibernating bears—they've since gone back to using telazol, which may take longer to wear off, but that seems fine for a bear that wants to sleep anyway. "Given the change in physiology, the lower body fat content—well, it just might not be the best choice for winter," Wolfe said of BAM, noting that it is used in summer months when appropriate—and that it's a great drug under the right circumstances.

"This is obviously not what we wanted to happen," Breck said.

AND WHAT'S the worst or most dangerous part of the job? When I asked this question, I was met with fast responses—unlike explaining their career motivation, this appears to be an easy question for the scientists to answer. Their responses:

Sharon Baruch-Mordo: "Not the bears. Avalanche danger."

Lisa Wolfe: "I-70 is by far the most dangerous part of my job."

And Dave Lewis? For him, the hardest part is "The Wagar Building." (Referring to the time he has to sit at a desk at Colorado State. Everyone else on the team jokes that they hope he has to sit there and atrophy for a while, since his stamina, strength, and ability to go enormous distances through deep snow tire everyone else out.)

Still, no one wants injuries from a bear, either—that would be bad for all parties involved and bad for research and research funding. To this end, they do a lot of training—practice handling bears, for instance. And on each trip, one or two people are avalanche certified and have wilderness training.

And as far as bear danger—well, no one seems worried. John Broderick had his middle finger (which he showed me) swiped by a bear cub, but that's the only injury anyone knows of.

"In fact," Lisa Wolfe said, "bears are hard to find, even when I'm *looking*. It's *hard* to attract bears." She noted that the team often burns honey on a small stove to attract bears—and even then, it can be hard work. "When we're out free-darting bears, it's really hard to get close enough."

"Bears just want to be left alone," someone said, and the group nodded in agreement.

And the best part of the job? Everyone indicated it's the fieldwork. The time spent with bears. And the camaraderie that develops in the process. I could see how they joked with each other, the way Baruch-Mordo was happy when Dave mentioned "Bear #4" or Broderick laughed when someone said, "Remember that time when we were on our knees and the bear started popping her teeth…"

In fact, it was great to see them all interact. "This research links people together between all the years," Broderick said. "When you're out in these elements, you come together. Many things have changed. Beacons, trapping technology, the research questions themselves."

But fondness for individual bears doesn't seem to change, and although they're supposed to refrain from giving the bears names, as is protocol for researchers, Wolfe admitted that everyone just ends up calling them by the number, but with the same fondness and tone of voice you'd use for a name. It's hard, basically, not to become attached.

And so, of course, there have been individual bears they've rooted for, "Old Boar" being one of them. They described him as "…an old gummer bear, an old guy in our study, a big old guy." He was captured in Aspen and moved to Craig, and later showed up at an airport in Wyoming—a huge distance to travel. The Wyoming officials decided to euthanize him, one reason being that he was old and his teeth worn.

"Ah, but he was so healthy and fat," Breck said.

"Yeah, he was doing just fine," Wolfe chimed in.

"We all wanted him to make it," Breck added.

"Everyone was rooting for him," Lewis agreed.

There was also the "Giant Left Hand Turn Bear," which was a fascinating look at bear's instinctual ability to navigate. This particular sow was blind in one eye. Using a GPS device to track it, they could see how, after being taken from Aspen to north of Rifle, she went back home again—a fairly short distance as the crow flies. But being blind in one eye, she made a huge circle—Rifle, Craig, almost to Steamboat, to Glenwood Canyon, Roaring Fork—one giant left-hand turn. "Considering the nutritional stress, the incredible trek, and the bad food year," Broderick said, "it's amazing that she had a cub. But have a cub she did."

Baruch-Mordo got out a map so we could see her trek—marveling at the huge distances she traveled to get home and den up.

And then there were the quiet, tender moments. Dave, for instance, told me of one of his favorite bear moments: "It was a hot summer day above Aspen and I was tracking our largest collared boar. By tracking I mean 'wimp-tracking,' with electronic equipment. I was stumbling through the brush toward the point where the bear had been about twelve hours earlier. I came to a ten-foot cliff separating myself from the bear's point and looked down to find a small male bear lounging in the exact spot the large bear had been twelve hours earlier. He was lying in the sun on his back like a human would sprawl out for sunny nap. I watched him for about ten minutes while he fussed and adjusted into more comfortable positions. Finally the air brought my presence to the bear's knowledge. I saw him freeze and start to scan for me with his eyes. Finally he found what he was looking for, he flipped over and shot through the brush in the opposite direction. Any day I can watch a bear out in the woods taking care of the bear necessities is a good day."

And then, too, are various bears' endearing characteristics. Lisa Wolfe, for instance, often finds herself rooting for mother bears. She recounted one instance in which she wanted to tranquilize the mother bear, but the mother was cuddling the cubs and wouldn't set them down. The cubs thus were in the way—preventing a good angle for the dart. Wolfe ended up crawling right up to the bear, taking the extension off her jab pole, and waiting for the bear, who was rocking the babies, to more or less rock into the needle and jab herself in the forearm.

Wolfe is enamored of how clever the mothers are about protecting their cubs. "I don't know what those mother bears are saying," she continued, "but if they bark a certain way, those cubs go *right* up a tree, and I mean right up. No messing around." (And here, we joked about wishing that human children listened as well.) "I've seen it time after time. A bear would rather have the cubs go up the tree and then draw you away. They'll do the killdeer thing [pretend to be injured, thus being easy prey]. It's really interesting from a biology standpoint, seeing what they have to do. But it also makes me sorry for what I have to do—all this handling of bears."

INDEED, IT SEEMS that this team of researchers wouldn't handle bears if they didn't need to—but the knowledge gained has been important to the bears' future. Originally, Broderick told me, the goal was to discover more about the basic ecology of bears. The technology was rudimentary or nonexistent. Over time, technology changed: VHF collars, the development of GPS, downloadable GPS, and then satellite GPS.

Traps developed from a basic snare to a box trap. Studies have changed too, and now often focus on bear-human interface. ("I can tell you bear stories," Baruch-Mordo told me, "but I can tell you even more dumpster stories"—and they joked about how well they know the dumpsters and alleys in Aspen, which is where much of their research takes place.)

The future of wildlife ecology, they agreed, will focus on human-wildlife interaction. There are still discoveries to be made, and the natural sciences component will always exist as part of the job. But often, these researchers said, their jobs are about "data points and models," mainly geared at the human-bear conflicts (which will only be on the rise, all agreed), and certainly, there will always be a lot of paperwork and desk-sitting involved.

But they all still look forward to what they call "good, honest work" out in the field. "Most wildlife professionals are about numbers and harvest quotas," Breck told me. "And that will always be central to the profession. But the vast majority of us want to be out in the field, too." By which he meant: Outside, with the bears.

The Beck Factor

A Conversation with Tom Beck

I'd wager that no one in Colorado knows bears better than Tom Beck. He's crawled into hundreds of dens where black bears lay sleeping, he's poked and prodded bears, tracked and followed bears, written and given talks about bears. He conducted the first significant studies of bears, and he's had an enormous influence on how they're studied today. As the bear biologist for Colorado Parks and Wildlife for twenty-five years—and his tenure there was not without controversy—he became, even in retirement, the person people turn to. "Talk to Beck," people will tell you if you ask about bears. "You gotta talk to Beck."

And so I did. As a person who "takes retirement seriously," he's about as easy to find as a shy Colorado bear. He's usually outdoors, not easily track-able. He doesn't have email and he lives in the most remote, hard-to-get-to corner of the state. But in the end, just as with a bear, a person can find him by being quietly patient.

Beck, although he's too humble to admit it, is widely known as "Colorado's black bear expert." He didn't know that would be the case back in 1978, when he initiated the first significant studies of bears—which he did only because, as he said, "I didn't want to study deer." When he was hired, he noted, there were a dozen people researching deer, but there'd been no work done on bears or cougars. "The hunting season was running from April to November—wide open," he told me. "We had absolutely no information on the density or distribution on bears, nor did we know how this hunting season was impacting the bears. At that time, bears were sort of on the same level with the coyote—vermin, nuisances. People could kill them however they wanted, whenever they wanted, more or less. But then there started to be more interest in black bears. Remember, we'd just come through a decade of the great changes in environmental laws, and demographics were changing."

Beck gazed into the future and worried: "I said to my boss, 'There aren't any controversies brewing right now, but there will be. And wouldn't it be nice if we had good data when the controversy starts?'" And indeed, by the early 1980s, Colorado Parks and Wildlife (CPW) was coming under scrutiny for its management program—the controversies had started sooner than even Beck had predicted.

Luckily, his first study was underway—although it was, to my mind, crazily and almost laughably difficult. First, CPW needed to close an area from hunting in order to be able to study the bears, which proved to be highly unpopular. They finally decided on the Black Mesa area, which had a high and real avalanche danger, and wasn't the best habitat for bears, so that meant there was a lot of ground to cover in order to find the creatures. This, then, is where the term "The Mutants" came into being—as Beck fondly refers to the team he built.

"The Mutants evolved as part of that project," he told me. "The only way you can do that kind of hard work is to have a good crew to help you. Fortunately, there were grizzly and black bear studies just starting up, so I recruited people from other studies who had experience. I wanted people who could flat-out work in the field, people who were in tip-top physical condition. Most worked out good, and we had a high retention rate. We were rough-looking, played real hard, and we bent and broke a lot of bureaucratic rules because we wanted to get the job done. There was stuff like carrying around stinking bear bait, but mainly it was the physical capabilities, day in day out. George Bock, a district wildlife manager, once said, 'You and that group are a bunch of mutants, you run everyone else in the ground.' Then it became a badge of honor. Kind of a twisted thing. We were hiking around in high-top Converse shoes, shorts—definitely not what the agency wanted us to look like. There was a perverse kind of pride in what we were capable of doing."

And what did these early studies reveal? For one thing, they confirmed that the researchers had a difficult time ahead of them—bears in Colorado are a low-density animal, with a bear per square mile at best. Another discovery had to do with bears' ranges. "One of the big things we learned was how much territory they cover," Beck said. "They have huge, huge ranges, and they make big daily movements. Still, I find that people don't understand how big these ranges are." He explained that there once was a theory separating "low country bears" from "high country bears," but that proved untrue. A good portion of the bears are coming down the mountains, then going right back up, often traveling forty miles in a day. "We documented those movements," Beck said. "We also learned a lot of basic stuff—when are the mothers having cubs, how many, stuff like that." They learned other things too—bears in southwest Colorado tend to be bigger, for instance; and conifer habitat, which is extensive in Colorado, is "darn near useless to a bear. We have a lot of it. It's poor habitat. We learned the value of oak-brush and aspen community."

Another impact these early studies had was less tangible,

but highly important: Beck and gang were able to change the public perception of bears. "Early on, bears didn't have a lot of respect within our agency or with hunters," Beck noted. "They did have the respect of the general public, although there wasn't that much information about them. We tried to elevate the general standing of the bears. To get people to see them in a positive light. We got a lot of press coverage at the time." Which is to say, I think, that the current healthy population of Colorado bears has a lot to do with Beck.

Beck's most memorable bear is a heartbreaker of a story. "Stumpy," Beck said, when I ask him to tell me about a bear. "Stumpy, for sure. Stumpy has kept me up many a night."

As it turned out, Stumpy also changed the way bear studies are done in the state.

The story is as difficult to hear as it is for Beck to tell. "We were using leg-hold snares, which were state of the art at that time," Beck said, "but the bears in Colorado are wary, and they fought the snare. They would chew toes off and break their legs." Here, he paused. "You have to understand, we loved these animals, we didn't want to see them hurt."

In the first year of the study, they caught a yearling female in a snare, where she sustained a compound facture on her left arm. They splinted her arm the best they could and released her, hoping for the best. In the fourth year of the study, they caught her again—her left foot was missing. This time, they'd caught her by the right foot. "She had fought so hard that she'd literally nearly severed it off, and in fact, we had to cut a few tendons and finish the job," Beck said quietly. "We put a collar on her, which she pulled off. But we got one on her cub, which is how we found her in the den that winter, and her foot was completely healed up. Now she had two stubs. She raised cubs, covered that hillside, though." In the end, he thinks she was killed by natural events, in a landslide that occurred in 1986, noting that "she lived a—I won't say a normal life, it impaired her, for sure—but she lived okay. I came away with this impression of how strong and tough and resilient and powerful these animals are."

But more than that, it made Beck reconsider what he was doing. "That bear made me reexamine everything," he said. "I had to ask myself, why are we doing this? Is the information we're getting worth it? Because there's a cost. Wildlife managers in general ignore those costs, especially when they're not that visible. But this was visible. And we wanted to make *darn sure* that nothing we were doing was frivolous. We ended that study early. We ended soon after that bear. I couldn't deal with the injuries. I don't think we're learning enough of value to continue the injuries. I said, 'Let's call it quits.' Which we did. 'I will never snare another bear,' I told my boss. 'Never.'"

Six years later, when Beck was reassigned to bears, he repeated his dictate. "I said, 'I won't snare another bear, so you gotta give me the money to design and build better traps.'"

His boss did, and Beck got enough money get forty-five big cage traps. "They worked fabulously," Beck said. "We never had another injury. The injury rate literally dropped to zero."

In addition to changing traps, Beck also went public about the injury rates, much to the chagrin of some: "I was told not to publish this stuff, it will cause trouble with the 'anti's.' But I did, and I got a colleague to publish his injury rates, too. People didn't want to talk about it. But we needed to. It really made me look at my profession, and some behaviors that I didn't like, which basically was the cavalier attitudes toward animals. I hunt and fish, and I have a lot of respect for the animals, and I think everyone else should too. This forced me to speak out. Which led to my high level of unpopularity within some of the agency. Some people liked what I was saying, and another bunch wanted me to shut up or get run over by a truck or something." Here, he paused. "I was comfortable with that."

THE MORE Beck studied bears, the more he came to respect them. "You come away with all this for a real respect for what bears are capable of," he said. "I studied crayfish, and I have a great respect for crayfish, but bears are something different. To see the way they can survive, even with physical injuries. The fabulous system of hibernation they have—they give birth, produce milk, raise young, don't lose much muscle strength—what a phenomenal adaptation to the world they live in! I also appreciate the way they use their noses to navigate; the way they teach their young."

He's impressed, too, with their ability to adapt. In the 1970s, Colorado's bear population was at a low point, Beck said, "mostly because of predator control—the poisoning, shooting and trapping from the end of World War II to the mid-seventies. But then the culture shifted, and Americans decided they didn't want to go to out and kill off all the predators." He added that there have also been massive changes in land use in the last thirty years—meaning, mainly, fewer domestic sheep. "There are multiple reasons for that," Beck said. "Look at ski resorts, for example—nearly all of them are built on sheep ranches. That took the constant pressure off the bears, and the bears, after some decades, built back up their populations."

There's no doubt that Beck has accomplished a great deal, both for humans and for bears. As *Ghost Grizzlies* author David Petersen, Beck's long-time friend put it: "Perhaps the most apt description I've ever heard of this complex fellow named Tom Beck came years ago from a fellow CPW biologist who referred to Tom as 'an intellectual in overalls.' Perfect! In fact Tom was raised in the swamps of interior Florida and still manifests some entertaining 'redneck' characteristics. Yet he is among the most intelligent, well-read, ethical and all-around wise men I've ever known. Within his profession, Tom Beck is widely acclaimed as one of the two leading black bear experts in the lower 48, the other being Lynn Rogers of the North American Bear Center in Ely, Minnesota."

Looking back on his career, Beck said, "I feel blessed to become a so-called expert. What an honor. I loved working with the bears, and I owe something back to the bears. They paid a price for the studies."

One can only assume that he's at least broken even, if not come out ahead. And I imagine that he'll soon be heading back into the mountains, which, like the bears, is where he belongs.

Beyond Bear Aware

The Future of Bears in Colorado

Bryan Peterson is a man on a mission, of that I'm sure. That he's called "The Bear Guy" by folks in his hometown is no surprise, but probably an understatement; I'd probably call him "The Friendly-Fanatical Bear Protector of the Universe." I considered this as he showed me highly sophisticated computer maps he's made of human-bear encounters, letters he's written to the city council, photos from his "trail cams," and—my favorite—a florescent orange "ticket" he's designed, which reads, "This is a Howdy partner message from a friendly bear smart Durango volunteer and the city of Durango…" and "Don't trash bears. Remove the food source—and you'll remove the bear."

Helping people and bears coexist—that's his main mission, and the mission of his organization, Bear Smart Durango. As the executive director, Peterson is joined by his dog, and they seem to be one-man, one-dog, pittance-paid team. They're also an enormous force of energy for the bears (and they have a cadre of volunteers, too). Their goal? To offer *real* solutions for bear-human conflicts by addressing the root causes. He furrowed his brow as he said to me, "Look, one way to approach this is the status quo—to relocate or put down bears.

But what communities *really* need to do is ask themselves what they can do to remove the attractants in the first place." Which is, as he explained, more complicated than it sounds.

ALTHOUGH BLACK BEARS still occupy vast areas of North America, bears have lost ninety percent of their original range. This holds true for Colorado bears as well, and they increasingly are finding houses in their habitat. In fact, human-bear conflicts are related to a third of all bear mortalities in the state—and in Durango area, eleven percent of all black bear deaths can be attributed to conflicts with people—including euthanizing of "problem" bears, gunshots from landowners, road deaths, electrocutions, and so on.

Bears will follow their instinct, and look for the easiest, highest-calorie food possible. Because they are large omnivores in need of lots of energy, bears are nearly always on a search for wild food sources—berries, insects, acorns, forbs, plants and carrion. They are especially in need of high-calorie food in the late summer and the fall, and that's when many bears move down from the mountains to oakbrush habitat to seek out acorns and berries. At this time, bears will feed for about twenty hours a day when berries are abundant, and they may consume up to thirty pounds of them a day (that's a lot of chokecherries!). Durango, and towns like it, have been built in the primary fall feeding area of bears, who have been feeding in these areas for thousands of years—and who have no other high-energy food sources available.

So when people fail to store garbage, pet food, or bird feeders properly, bears will find those sources of food. They're hungry and they're smart, and once they've figured out a food source, they become food-conditioned, and this unwanted bear behavior will continue throughout the life of the bear—about twenty-five years.

Bears will do what bears do—it's *people's* behavior that needs to change. Peterson believes it's the responsibility of residents who choose to live in bear habitat to learn to live respectfully with bears. And what does that come down to? Mainly, trash.

Storing trash well may sound like an "of course" no-brainer, but it's not so simple. Unlikely culprits are everywhere. Peterson told me, for example, of a homeless man who was bitten in Durango—the bear was becoming habituated to food sources outside the food kitchen. Another cub was hit by a car—Peterson showed me a photo of the bloody cub. After getting permission from Colorado Parks and Wildlife (CPW) to keep the bear, Peterson took it to a taxidermist and helped skin it out; in the stomach, he found walnut chicken salad and French green beans—the bear, he knew, was crossing the highway to eat at a natural food store. "I've had enough of that chicken salad to know where it came from," he said, noting that he's now using the cub as a learning tool. Peterson also told me about friends of his—environmentally aware friends who know of his work—and even *they* put out trash into non-bearproof containers. Which is just to say: Even people who are doing good things—running homeless shelters, operating health food stores, and friends who know better—are still culpable. It strikes me that it's not just a problem of the occasional brainless jerk—keeping food sources away from bears is more problematic than we think.

Consider, for example, that prime bear habitat, between 6,000 and 9,500 feet in altitude, also happens to be prime condo and second-home habitat. People at these locations like to keep their windows open at night for the breeze, they have pets, they have birdfeeders, and they produce trash. They simply may not be willing to do some of the activities required (locking lower-story windows, keeping bird feeders inside, putting away dog food, storing trash well). And, as is often the case, they're not there regularly enough to know the codes and rules. On top of that, it's more than homeowners that need education—after all, many Colorado mountain towns have a mix of second (or third) homes; service industry employees, who often do not speak English as their first language; residents; businesses; and tourists. Getting to all these various groups is a bit of a task.

And yet: Reducing conflict is so *easy*—remove the attractive nuisances and the bears will stay away. The solution to most bear-human conflict is so basic, and that's the basic frustration expressed by most of the folks I talked to. Huge differences can be made, for example, by simply timing the take-out of the trash. One 1994 study found that homes that left trash out overnight were visited by bears 70% of the time, but when trash was put out the morning, only 2% were visited by bears. Peterson finds plenty of people who insist they need to put out the trash the night before—which is why, perhaps, educating people simply isn't enough. Education surely goes a long way (after getting one of Peterson's orange tickets on my trash can, I'd probably laugh at the humor—and then change my ways), and education should continue. But in the end, education is simply not enough.

Sharon Baruch-Mordo, a postdoctoral researcher at Colorado State University, agrees. She offered a helpful analogy—she compared becoming "bear smart" to obeying the DUI or seatbelt-wearing laws. Education is certainly part of the key, but eventually there needs to be enforcement and fines. Peterson couldn't agree more. "Education will only take you so far. We need a mechanism to change people's behavior. And yes, that means fines." Every CPW and bear person I talked to while writing this book said nearly the same thing—we need a way to ticket, to enforce, and to force people into being smart. Peterson adds that Tom Beck once told him, "You'll try education for five years or so. You'll hear every excuse in the book. Then you're going to need enforcement."

This is why the various "bear smart" campaigns (CPW's is called "bear aware") around the state, which offer advice to reduce conflicts, may not be working all that well. The signs posted in outdoor bathrooms and the notices in park bulletins—all that practical advice—are all good and well. We're reminded over and over that garbage kills bears, that we should stow our trash in bear-proof containers, and that we should close and lock first-story windows and cars. But perhaps it's not until we have to pay some hard-earned cash that we might change our ways. And in the meantime, the bears die.

COLORADO PARKS AND WILDLIFE (CPW) has a clear "two-strikes policy" against "offender bears." This means that the first time a bear causes trouble and is captured it is ear-tagged; if a bear is captured a second time, that's a death sentence. And killing a bear is not an action that wildlife officials relish. "Putting down bears is my least favorite thing I have to do. I absolutely hate it," Kevin Wright, a CPW manager, told me. I heard the same from other CPW employees, who noted that they didn't get into the business to kill bears. (As an aside, often the hides of such bears are sold at public auction, but the gall bladders are destroyed to keep them off the black market.)

Even if they relocate a bear, that's not always successful. Sometimes, Wright explained, they can run out of suitable habitat. Peterson agreed. He told me that he went along with CPW officials to view a captured, large, male black bear. "I found its skeleton five years later—same ear tag. It had traveled a great distance to get back to its home range only to be hit by a car. This is a perfect example of how bear relocation fails. It works for young males because they travel so much, but others want their home range. They're going to try to get home, and they're going to get killed on the way."

There are many reasons why relocating bears is problematic. One is that the transplanted bear has a disadvantage when it comes to finding food—since much of a bear's activities are based on memory and learning. It's also expensive in both dollars and manpower. "Most importantly," Tom Beck noted, "moving bears only treats the symptoms, not the problem of access to human food."

That's why Peterson isn't satisfied with the status quo—putting down bears and relocating them have their places, but these actions aren't really solving any problems.

EVERYONE I talked to in Colorado agreed that 2007 was a bad year. It seemed as if bears were taking over the state; and indeed, there were more bear-human conflicts than in any other recorded year. Statewide, 418 bears died in conflicts with people. Unsurprisingly, this coincided with a bad drought year. Peterson noted, "Problems with black bears typically begin in bad natural food years," adding that bears are curious and intelligent, and "have great memories for locations of food sources, both in the wild and in urban areas."

But in 2008, bears enjoyed a banner year for natural foods. The incidences of conflicts went way down, suggesting that the bears returned to their natural habitat (although it's important to note that many problem bears had been removed). Many believe, however, that the saying "a fed bear is a dead bear" isn't quite true. Once food sources are available, bears will return to natural habitat.

When considering consumption of human food, there's also another factor to take into account—the individual bear's health. After all, we humans aren't known for healthful eating, Peterson told me two stories that illustrate the difference—one was of a young bear in a tree, sleeping all the time.

"This bear was sick from eating the grease from the Dairy Queen," he noted, showing me a picture of a bear that did, indeed, look sick. But then he told me about one of his bear encounters in the wild: "Man, that bear was huge. I had a remote trail cam, and I walked out to check it, and I saw a huge bear very close eating serviceberries. He was woofing and snorting, spitting out the debris. That was a cool bear. That bear taught me not to dismiss black bears. He was big and healthy and strong."

All this begs the question of the future of bears in Colorado. As a species, they're doing fine. But one wonders if the bear-human conflict is only going to get worse if, as predicted, drought years become more common. New studies are tracing how climate change is gradually changing the timing of the seasons. In Colorado, for example, some plant species have started flowering earlier in the spring. There's also the effect of pinebark beetle infestations, coniferous forests turning to aspens, and warmer winters to consider. What all this means to the bears isn't yet known, but I'm guessing that "bear smarts" are going to get essential.

Peterson's typical day starts early and ends late, at least from about April 15 to November 15. "As soon as there's light in the sky, we start out," he said ("we" meaning him and his dog). For the next two hours (while there's light but it's too early for residents to have picked up their trash), Peterson is driving around, patrolling Durango and its environs. He documents trash cans that have been knocked over or been visited by bears and takes photos. "People kept saying we didn't have a problem, so I went out and documented the problem. Now it's obvious there's a problem."

How do people know that bears have been there—and not dogs or raccoons? "It's usually obvious," he said. "For one thing, we often see tracks, or the bear itself, or scat. Plus bears trash stuff in a particular way"—and here he showed me many, many pictures of trash scattered around, often pulled into the underbrush.

After driving around, Peterson passes violations on to the police or city code enforcement staff—he has them on speed dial—and then he goes home to type up a report and log all the bear sightings and incidents. His work, though, has just started. The list of his accomplishments thus far is long: He advocated for getting city and county wildlife ordinances passed. He's also designed and printed materials, such as the orange ticket he (and other volunteers) place on trashcans. He's also makes sure bears get newspaper coverage—he noted, for example, that often people don't know if bears are being killed, and if they don't know, they aren't aware there's a problem. He's also encouraged the city to get bear-resistant trash cans, which they've made available. He writes fundraising letters, writes a column for the newspaper for six months of the year, talks to elementary school students and other groups, he does print and radio education for Fort Lewis College, and has a Bear Smart booth at farmers' markets. He's also turned May into "Be Bear-Smart Month." His plans are just as varied: bringing in a bear expert once a year, putting together a review of the trash ordinance to see what the city has learned and what residents can do better, and to have an education push in mid-April when the ordinances go into effect each year. Not all bear smart has to be serious—and Peterson mentioned his plan to have an "Open Mic Bear Night," where people could come and tell their bear stories. In Durango, he noted, there will be no shortage of stories.

What does he get paid? Not much. Pats on the back.

"Why do you do this?" I asked him. I'm not only thinking of all the lost hours of sleep, but the fact that his work is not without its dangers—he's been charged several times by bears guarding their trash, and he's been harassed by people who don't appreciate getting violation notices, or who think he's spying.

"Good question," he said. "I ask myself that all the time. People sometimes ask me, 'What makes you qualified?' to which I say, 'There are other people far more qualified. But they're not doing it. Someone needs to do this.'"

When he started, he hoped he would do this work for ten years. But the conflict hasn't stopped, so he hasn't either. "I'm happy with what we've done—the two ordinances especially—but if you look at whether there's really been a reduction in conflict, well, there's no way you'd conclude we've been successful yet." Then he paused and added, "I get tired of hearing the same stories. I have no problem with killing bears if it's a last resort. But if you're killing bears—and no one is doing anything [to prevent those deaths]—well, that's just not right."

And how long is he going to keep doing this? When I asked him, he reached over to pet his dog and said, "We'll keep doing it until it doesn't need to be done."

Basic Bear Smarts

It's good to know—or be reminded of—the basics:

- Place garbage in a secure building or a bear-resistant trash can or dumpster. If you don't have a place to store garbage, ask the trash company for a bear-resistant container, or order one.
- Place smelly food scraps in the freezer until garbage day.
- Rinse out all cans, bottles and jars so that they are free of food and odors before putting them out for recycling or pickup.
- Put out garbage cans only on the morning of pickup—*not* the night before.
- Wash garbage cans regularly with ammonia to eliminate food odors.
- Don't leave pet food or pet dishes outside. Store food in an odor-free container.
- Use bird feeders only from November until the end of March, when bears are hibernating. These are a major cause of wildlife conflicts. In addition to bears, feeders may also attract small mammals, deer, and mountain lions. Birds do not need to be fed during the summer—attract birds naturally with hanging flower baskets, putting out a bird bath or planting a variety of flowers.
- If bears get into bird feeders, take the feeders down immediately and don't put them back up.

- Pick ripe fruit from trees and off the ground.
- Clean outdoor grills after each use; the smell of grease can attract bears.
- Never intentionally feed bears.
- Close and lock lower floor windows and doors of your house.
- Clean up thoroughly after outdoor parties.
- Don't leave food in your car, lock car doors. Bears are smart and many have learned to open car doors.
- When camping, store food and garbage inside a locked vehicle. Keep the campsite clean. Don't eat in the tent. In the backcountry, hang your food at least 10 feet high and 10 feet away from anything a bear can climb.
- Bears are not naturally aggressive toward people and prefer to avoid contact. If you see a bear in your neighborhood make it feel unwelcome: yell at it, throw sticks and rocks at it. But never approach a bear.

About the Author

Laura Pritchett is the author/editor of six books. Her fiction includes the novels *Sky Bridge* and *Hell's Bottom, Colorado*; her three anthologies include *Pulse of the River, Home Land,* and *Going Green: True Tales from Gleaners, Scavengers, and Dumpster Divers.* Pritchett frequently writes about the West and her home state of Colorado, and has published over 100 essays and short stories in numerous magazines, including *The Sun, Orion, OnEarth, Poets & Writers, High Country News, 5280,* and on the National Public Radio series *This I Believe,* and others. Her work has received numerous awards, including the PEN USA Award, the Colorado Book Award, and the Milkweed National Fiction Prize. See more about her at www.laurapritchett.com.